Advance Praise for *Selling to China*

"Chao has produced an indispensable guidebook for those interested in doing business with China and a valuable resource for anyone seeking greater understanding of contemporary Chinese thinking and behavior."

—Burton Levin, former US ambassador to Burma and US consulate general in Hong Kong

"Tightly written . . . entertaining account of real-world business tactics and strategy, rather than just another boring business book."

—*Kirkus Reviews*

"A useful book aimed at serious entrepreneurs to enter the China market."

—*Library Journal*

"This is the best text on doing business in China. It's practical, insightful, and all-inclusive. Every CEO, businessperson, and anybody interested in China should read it. The unique experiences Mr. Chao shares can save years of trial and error, not to mention the costs.

—Yupin Wang, former IBM director

"Selling to China . . . is a timely, relevant read for SMB owners who think they're read~~~ ~~~ is a thinker and strategist whose b~~~~~~~~~~~~~~~~~~~~~~~~~predict your chances [in China]."

eader Views

"The book will be most informative to all who wish to be successful in China. Chao's writing style is to the point and covers a wealth of valuable advice and real-life case studies. This should be required reading for all businesspeople wanting to go to China."

—Vincent Cook, former chief operating officer at
IBM Asia-Pacific Corporation

"Stanley Chao will save small- and medium-sized business owners and managers a great deal of time and trouble when they do business in China. Selling to China is a welcome and timely guidebook by an expert who tells it like it is."

—*ForeWord Clarion Reviews*

Selling to China

A Guide to Doing Business in China
for Small- and Medium-Sized Companies

STANLEY CHAO

iUniverse, Inc.
Bloomington

Selling to China
A Guide to Doing Business in China for Small- and Medium-Sized Companies

iUniverse books may be ordered through booksellers or by contacting:

iUniverse
1663 Liberty Drive
Bloomington, IN 47403
www.iuniverse.com
1-800-Authors (1-800-288-4677)

ISBN: 978-1-4759-1178-7 (sc)
ISBN: 978-1-4759-1180-0 (e)

Library of Congress Control Number: 2012917382

Printed in the United States of America

iUniverse rev. date: 10/23/2012

To my parents who gave me the foundation.

To my wife who gave me the inspiration.

*And to my children, May and Michael,
who gave me the motivation.*

Contents

Introduction

This book is written for and dedicated to the many small- and medium-sized businesses (SMBs) either thinking of or already doing business in China. In light of the changes that have marked the past ten years or so—China's entry into the World Trade Organization, the growth of the Internet, the rise of China's middle class, and Beijing's willingness to open its business borders to the rest of the world—SMBs today enjoy the same opportunities in China that were once only granted to the large multinational conglomerates.

The conventional wisdom that only large corporations can do business in China is a thing of the past. While I was attending the UCLA Anderson School of Business in the midnineties, professors taught that only multinational organizations (MNOs) like IBM, Motorola, and Philips Electronics could afford the time, money, political connections, and multiple failures required to stick it out in China. Companies had to lose millions before seeing initial profits. In short, you had to pay your dues first—no pain, no gain.

Indeed, China is still the Wild West and far from meeting our Western standards with respect to business ethics and laws. But it has also come a long way, and it now possesses the basic economic building blocks: a growing middle class, a Western-educated workforce fluent in English, a relatively advanced banking and financial infrastructure, and—most important—a semi-market-driven economy that will someday surpass that of the United States. China's economy is accelerating at speeds we have not seen since the nineteenth-century Industrial Revolution. China's voracious appetite for products, technologies, and services is growing so fast that the MNOs are unable to keep up. Ultimately, it will be the thousands of foreign SMBs, who are nimbler and more innovative, picking up the slack.

Back in the United States, SMBs are also facing a new economic landscape that forces them to look elsewhere for customers. The recent economic and financial meltdown, which picked up steam in 2008 and 2009, has put a financial stranglehold on the American consumer. And this could last for several more years as we continue to see real-estate prices fall and a lack of job creation. To survive, SMBs will be forced to look toward other markets: to China and its 1.3 billion consumers, to India (which already boasts the world's second-largest Internet market), and to Brazil, which has joined the world's stage by hosting the 2014 World Cup and 2016 Olympics. China, viewed before as only a low-cost manufacturing supply center, will now offer SMBs a new market opportunity with a growing middle class and a thirst for Western products. China's population, unlike that of Japan and the United States, is increasingly young and affluent. The World Bank estimates that China will have 53 percent of the world's middle class by 2030, roughly 700 million people. And because China's younger generation is more educated than its seniors, the wealthiest consumers will be between the ages of twenty-four and forty-four, as compared to the United States where incomes peak between ages forty-five and fifty-four.

MNOs have sowed seeds in China since the 1970s, and most, if not all, already have solid footholds in the country. SMBs, however, are just making the transition as they rely less on the American consumer and more on the world's demand for plasma televisions, automobiles, branded clothing, and industrial-related equipment. The struggle for foreign SMBs, however, will be a more difficult road when compared to MNOs that are rich with cash, manpower, and international experience. With limited resources, language abilities, and cross-cultural exposure, they'll need external support. And so it is the purpose of my efforts as a China business consultant and this book to assist the SMBs in solving the mysteries and inconsistencies of China. Inevitably, all businesses, big or small, will be international.

SMBs may think they need at least $500 million in annual revenue and two thousand employees to enter the China market. This is no longer true. Opportunities in China are abundant for fast-moving, flexible, and resourceful SMBs. I have consulted for start-ups seeking outsourcing opportunities in the medical disposables market, developed a market-entry strategy for a ten-employee company with barely a few hundred thousand dollars in sales, and sold scientific analytical software for three computer scientists working out of their garages. Some succeeded; others did not. Don't get me wrong—China is still not for everybody, but today's China opens opportunities to smaller companies that were not available just ten or fifteen years ago.

I see so few books about doing business in China for SMBs. Indeed, there are excellent books about China, but they cater only to the Fortune 1000—or at least companies with hundreds of millions of dollars in annual revenue. It's interesting to read about the adventures and problems that McDonald's, Starbucks, and Warren Buffett face in China. As a China watcher, it's good to know what they are doing and how they are solving their "China problems." But their world doesn't resonate well with the thousands of SMBs around the world wishing to get a crack at China. Big-company solutions and methods simply aren't practical for SMBs.

The SMBs I know and consult for usually share certain characteristics: they lack knowledge and experience in China, possess no political influence, have limited budgets, and must reach profitability in twenty-four months or less. Fortune 1000 companies are just the opposite: they can hire experienced China executives, spend tens of millions of dollars, plan five- to ten-year growth strategies, and schedule meetings with high-ranking Communist officials at their leisure.

Take Mattel, the world's largest toy manufacturer. They recalled millions of toys and wrongly accused their Chinese suppliers of poor quality, when in actuality, it was their own design flaws that had created the problems. How did they solve this mishap? Mattel's consulting company advised them to make a public apology directly to the Chinese government. With dozens of reporters and cameras rolling, a Mattel executive made a public apology face-to-face to Li Changjiang, China's chief quality watchdog who reports directly to China's President Hu Jiantao. This solution, though suitable for Mattel, would never have worked for SMBs. My clients, mostly companies with annual revenues between $10 million and $250 million, simply do not have access to China's ministry officials, nor would they have the same public exposure and publicity as Mattel. So SMBs need to find other means to solve their problems.

This book addresses the real, day-to-day problems in China faced by the SMBs. How do you draft a contract and enforce it knowing that your Chinese partner won't abide by it? How can you set up a local office with a limited budget? How will you find potential distributors and customers? I'll address these issues and give implementable and measurable solutions. Further, the solutions I offer have all been proven in the field by my consulting customers.

Much of the conventional wisdom about doing business in China will be debunked. Some of these truisms related to negotiations, social activities, and managing relations are important and should be followed when in China. But many of them are exaggerated and overplayed by consultants and in how-to books as if they were a matter of life and death. It is nice to know them and even practice them when in China, but they will not be the underlying reasons for your success. Success or failure will still be based on fundamentally sound business principles. Most foreign businesspeople have heard these old adages: Chinese people will be upset if you don't use chopsticks; the Chinese lack respect for intellectual property because of Confucian ideologies; and, my personal favorite, you can lose a deal if you handle Chinese people's business cards improperly. It's these comments that trivialize the complexities of China and make Chinese businesspeople seem wildly unreasonable, like they're from Mars. Foreign and Chinese businesspeople share a common goal and that's to make money, and neither side will let a little impoliteness or cultural ineptitude impede these goals. If someone truly lost a deal because he or she disrespected a Chinese businessperson's card, then my guess is that the business proposition was in peril from the beginning.

Businesspeople get bogged down by these dozens of little dos and don'ts—do drink, don't show your emotions, do give gifts, don't tell jokes—to the point that they feel unnatural and become people they are not for fear of offending their Chinese counterparts. And this is wrong. As a foreigner in China, you are already a fish out of water. You look and talk differently. Everybody knows you're a foreigner—so just be yourself and stop pretending to be Chinese. These cultural lessons are fine for the interested tourist, but they will not improve your chances of business success in China. There are bigger things to worry about, and this book addresses the more important matters.

My knowledge comes from two areas: working in Asia and China for Fortune 500 companies and then later, with my own consulting company, helping SMBs with their China strategies. It was a difficult transition. Smaller companies wanted things done differently; quantifiable results were demanded in months rather than years, budgets were thousands (instead of millions) of dollars, and there was little or no support staff. So, out of necessity, I became an expert in various functions: marketing, sales, Chinese law, and export licensing issues.

Besides the business experience, my family greatly contributed to my "Chinesification." I was born in the United States but grew up in a traditional Chinese family with three generations living under one roof. Growing up, I learned about Chinese culture and language from my grandmother. She didn't sit me down and teach me these things; rather, I learned from observing her. I watched her converse with her friends, noting the behaviors, gestures, and subtle nuances that made her Chinese. For example, she always asked my friends when they were visiting the house, "Have you eaten yet? Do you want something to drink?" Before they could even answer, she would run into the kitchen and come back with some Chinese bread or snacks. It took me twenty years to understand why she did this, as I am now asked the same question many times over in China.

Learning Chinese came free for me when I was a youngster, as my parents spoke little English. Even though I have degrees from prestigious American universities, I could not do what I do today without knowing Chinese. If I had used translators or had been required to listen to Chinese businesspeople's broken English, I would not have understood the "behind the scenes" discussions in meetings and would not have been able to differentiate a real yes from a polite one. I owe my parents and grandmother half my salary.

Although many inferences are made throughout the book regarding the Chinese government's inconsistencies in dealing with foreign companies as well as the sometimes subpar ethical behavior of Chinese businesspeople, in no way do I consider these to be inhibitions to doing business in China. On the contrary, these are simply new rules to an old game, and the game is to make money. I am just making first-timers to China aware of these new variables and advising them on ways to handle them and thrive in spite of them.

Also, my tone, at times, may seem condescending and critical of the Chinese. This is not my intention. In fact, I have the utmost respect for them, and the book is written not to scorn them but to try, in my small way, to bridge the gap between Western and Chinese cultures, languages, and histories. Many

Westerners label Chinese businesspeople as "black hearts" or "unscrupulous entrepreneurs." They are not. China is in the midst of its own industrial revolution. Many historians claim that what China is going through today—unfair labor practices, human rights violations, environmental pollution, poorly manufactured products, and tainted foods—were exactly the same issues that occurred in the United States during the nineteenth-century Industrial Revolution. Only this time, unsavory events are magnified by television, the Internet, and opinions from bloggers and cell phone users reporting in real time. Further, what happens in a small factory on the outskirts of Shenzhen can affect citizens living halfway around the world in Pocatello, Idaho.

China is also still in the recovery phase from self-inflicted catastrophes—the Cultural Revolution and the Great Leap Forward—Communist Party socio-political programs in which tens of millions of Chinese perished; and hundreds of millions more Chinese, even today, suffer the mental anguish and pain of China's past. I'm not making excuses for China, but these are indisputable facts. China needs time to catch up to the West. It will take time, and we will probably not see the end results for another generation or two. But I have faith that China, in time, will be equal to the West in human and equal rights, religious freedom, and ethical behavior. It is a very exciting time to be involved in doing business in China, and we are just now at the precipice, with SMBs poised to take part in the history being made. I hope you will join me in the adventure.

Chapter 1
Debunking Conventional Wisdom

One of the things I do with new consulting clients is give them a crash course on what to expect in China, especially if they have never been there. Of course, we'll discuss some of the basics: history, politics, law, culture, and business strategy. Invariably, I get odd questions: "Do Chinese wives have to walk three steps behind their husbands?" "Will monkey brain be served at our business dinner—and is it rude if I don't eat it?" "Should I not openly disagree with our Chinese partner so he can save face?" Though I have eaten some strange things—beaver, donkey testicles, scorpion, silkworms—I've never come across monkey brain. Other more conventional questions concerning *guanxi*, socializing, Confucianism, and trust come up as well.

My guess is that these queries came from embellished anecdotes, old Charlie Chan movies, or, even worse, from books written about China in the 1980s and '90s. After so many of these entertaining but disturbing questions, I want to finally set the record straight on these folklores.

This chapter will be devoted to debunking many of the half-truths and sweeping generalizations about China that oversimplify, trivialize, and don't do justice to how business is really conducted in China. Authors, Chinese experts, and consultants exaggerate the importance of these principles to the point that businesspeople become confused and lose track of what made them successful in the first place. When I interviewed Christopher Wright, the Australian government's senior trade commissioner based in Shanghai, he showed me a manual written by a consulting company that described dos and don'ts to observe while doing business in China. Using cartoon scenes, it was a serious attempt to describe cultural and behavior etiquette differences. One of the comic strips showed a foreign businessman fumbling for his business card in one hand while reaching for his Chinese partner's card with the other. A second scene has a foreigner taking notes on the Chinese person's card while the Chinese contingency looked on in obvious anger.

"It is material like this," says Wright, "that confuses foreigners. They mislead companies out of good common business sense and commercial practices into thinking that some black magic exists for success in China. It's all made up by these consultants. At the end of the day, practical business sense will determine if companies succeed in China—nothing more, nothing less. We lose focus, lose clarity, and dive into the black magic."

Many of the how-to books for MNOs stress certain mannerisms, behaviors, and proper etiquette. When General Electric's CEO meets a senior Communist Party official in Beijing, I agree that some of the conventional wisdom still applies: Everything said and done at this meeting is on record for all the world to see.

Indeed, it would be embarrassing for General Electric's CEO to be seen fumbling with his chopsticks or eating with a fork while others are using chopsticks. But SMBs will rarely face such pomp and circumstance, so don't fret if your chopsticks skills need improvement. For SMBs, much of the conventional wisdom does not apply, or at least it should not be a central focus in a meeting or relationship. At the end of the day, foreign businesspeople must be comfortable in their own skins and not always focused on trying to be people they are not or pleasing their Chinese counterparts. This unnatural behavior is a recipe for failure.

Guanxi: It's Not That Important

The term *guanxi* refers to a person's connections; in particular, it refers to people in influential or higher positions who would be willing to perform favors for you—knowing, however, that these favors will undoubtedly be reciprocated sometime in the future. Expressions like "I owe you one" or "I'll scratch your back if you scratch mine" are synonymous with guanxi.

The cultural difference is in the degree of the favors. In the West, we tend to use guanxi for something special or out of the ordinary, such as securing hard-to-get basketball tickets from an old friend, borrowing money from a family member, or asking a business associate for an interview for your son or daughter. In China, however, guanxi was a matter of life and death. The Chinese, having lived in poverty for the past two thousand years, used guanxi to get the basic necessities of life: food, clothing, and shelter. Without guanxi, you were alone, out to fend for yourself.

During Communism, anything that was in short supply or that needed an official's signature—entrance into college, a train

11

ticket, or a job—was obtained with guanxi. Having a relative or friend in high places meant a ticket to better government housing, a higher-paying job, and access to Friendship Stores where you could buy hard-to-find goods, such as Cadbury chocolates and American-made soap.

Similarly, foreign companies in the 1980s and '90s ran their China businesses based on guanxi rather than good, solid business practices. This is precisely why only the MNOs could lay claim to China at that time. Besides having money, they nurtured and captured guanxi over periods of five to ten years before seeing any concrete progress. Relationship building with the Communist officials who wielded all the business power at that time was slow and cumbersome.

My aunt who lives in Wuhan, a city in central China, gave me an example of how she used her guanxi. In the early 1970s, her son, just married, wanted to move out of the family apartment. Most Chinese at that time lived in government-owned apartments, and these were always in short supply, sometimes requiring a four- to five-year wait. My aunt, who had been an elementary school classmate of a Wuhan Communist Party official, had dinner with him and explained her son's situation. Over the next few months, she showered the official with gifts and food. Her son magically moved to the top of the list and was soon living in one of the better apartment complexes in the city.

Here's another example: In 1987 I went to Northeast University in Shenyang with my father, who was teaching a summer course in electrical engineering. The university sent a junior professor, Mr. Ding, to pick us up in Beijing, where we were to stay overnight before continuing to Shenyang. On the morning of our departure to Shenyang, the professor incessantly told us how he had waited at the train station all day to purchase our train tickets. He explained how difficult it was to obtain first-class tickets given the shortage of seats, and how he had to use his guanxi to get these prized "soft" seats (the cushioned seats that were only available in first class).

This continuous nagging went on the whole week. Everything Mr. Ding did for us required a lecture on how difficult it had been. "It took me five days to get the best rooms at the hotel for you. I went all the way across town to buy an overhead projector for your lectures." Why was he telling us all this? Did he want money? We found out two months later when we returned to the States: we became his guanxi. He wrote us letters asking us to sponsor his tourist visa to the United States and to send foreign engineering textbooks and English-language courses on tape. Later he pleaded with us to sponsor his children to attend American universities. His requests were never-ending.

Things are very different in China today. Guanxi just isn't that important anymore, or at least it is equal in importance to having connections in the West. The higher standards of living for millions of Chinese have reduced the necessity for guanxi. Food, shelter, and clothing are readily available to a growing Chinese middle class. There is certainly no short supply of airplane or train tickets unless one is traveling during the holidays, and then it might be advantageous to know someone at the Ministry of Railways.

Modern and updated laws and regulations in China have improved conditions over the past twenty years, thus reducing the need for guanxi. Though sometimes still backward, there are now procedures for getting things done. Take foreign travel as an example. Before, you needed guanxi with high government officials to obtain a foreign visa to travel abroad. Today, as long as you can show a return ticket and enough money to support the trip, you can go just about anywhere in the world. The same goes for applying for a driver's license, seeking medical attention, or registering a company.

The mobility of the Chinese is another reason for the lessening importance of guanxi. Before, Chinese families lived in their hometowns for hundreds of years, never moving. They knew their neighbors from many generations back. The guanxi was deeply rooted and uncompromising. Go to one of the big cities today, such as Shanghai or Guangzhou, and I'll guess it's a fifty-fifty split between locals and out-of-towners. This "transient" trend is a result of the central government's push to drive rural Chinese to the cities. Most of the migrants are young Chinese seeking a better life, and they are relying more on their education, intelligence, and self-reliant attitude to get ahead—not on traditional guanxi.

What lesson is there for SMBs? Don't let anybody tell you that guanxi is an absolute must for doing business in China. It's just not that important anymore. Of course, it won't hurt to have guanxi, and you might get things done faster or gain better contacts and meetings, but just like in the United States, diligence and tenacity will still pay off. At the end, the forces of business—product, price, quality, and competition—along with hard work, will decide your fate in China, not guanxi.

"I divide my customers into two groups: the older generation in their forties and above, and the Generation X group," says Gary

Chan, a twenty-five-year veteran of working in China and current general manager of Lenze Motors China, a German servo motor manufacturer with factories throughout China. "I need to build guanxi with my older customers with the traditional customs of dinners, karaoke, and small gifts. This means a lot to them. For my Generation X customers, I get business because we deliver good components, having nothing to do with guanxi. Regardless of my relations with them, they'll drop me if my pricing or quality is poor. Times are changing."

In 2005, my client, a medical imaging company, wanted to license its technology to Mindray, a Chinese medical company specializing in patient-monitoring and medical imaging equipment. I had no prior business with them and searched my Rolodex for contacts but to no avail. I then made phone calls to the Shenzhen headquarters and sent e-mails and faxes. No replies. I finally found a manager at their US headquarters. We met, but he didn't pass my business proposal on to the home office. This mindless searching for contacts went on for months.

But I wasn't about to give up. I went to Mindray's booth at the China International Medical Equipment Fair and found an executive who eventually set up a face-to-face visit for my client. Unfortunately, things did not work out between the companies as the American company's technology was priced too high for what the Chinese market could bear at that time, but it shows that hard work and diligence is just as good as guanxi. Having guanxi would have saved me a few months, but the results would have been the same.

Don't Lose Face over *Mianzi*

Mianzi or "face" is a very important concept for the Chinese. It's your reputation and how people look upon you. There are expressions in Chinese that allow a person to give, lose, save, or gain mianzi. Mianzi is not difficult for foreigners to understand, as we are keenly aware of our own and our colleagues' reputations. English expressions like "making me look bad" or "showing me off" carry the same meanings as mianzi. Mianzi, however, takes on much more importance for the Chinese, as they see it as one of the major focal points in any business meeting or relationship. For Westerners, mianzi takes a secondary position; it is not something they really think about once a meeting or relationship commences.

When doing business for my clients in China, I'm often confronted with the mianzi dilemma. I'm American Chinese, but I'm seen as a full-blown Chinese by my Chinese counterparts. They expect me to act Chinese, and the mianzi concept plays a big role in acting Chinese.

In the spring of 2007, I was searching for a new distributor for my client, an American enterprise software developer. I met with a small distributor in Shenzhen. After an hour of introductions, I doubted very much they could readily sell my client's software. I was ready to leave but could not just say, "You're too small a company and have no technical capabilities, so let's end this meeting now." For the sake of mianzi I begrudgingly spent the entire day with them exchanging pleasantries and asking them detailed questions about their company as if I were still interested in working with them. After dinner I had to finally refuse their karaoke invitation, and I went back to my hotel, upset that I had wasted the whole day.

Because I look and speak like a local Chinese, I feel obligated to act Chinese and make mianzi a priority in my Chinese relationships. MNOs must also do the same since they are usually dealing with large state-owned enterprises (SOE) where high-ranking Communist officials sit on the management teams. These Chinese statesmen are traditionalists and value the old ways. But I tell my SMB clients to not put mianzi in the forefront of any meetings or business relationships. In most cases the SMB's Chinese counterpart is also an SMB, and they are just like you: direct, short on time, and very pragmatic. The owner is probably young (in his or her forties) and would also prefer to dispense with the old customs.

In sum, don't get so immersed in mianzi that it takes away from your immediate purpose and goals. Don't be somebody that you're not. It's difficult to act Chinese, and the reality is that the Chinese don't expect you to act Chinese either. Be yourself, be polite, and be mindful of respecting your Chinese partner just as you do partners in the United States; but don't shy away from asking tough questions, cutting a meeting short, or abruptly ending a relationship. The Chinese will do the same to you.

Drinking and Socializing

Is all this drinking, eating, and singing absolutely necessary? Will the business relationship be affected if you don't attend these events? Conventional wisdom says yes. Most experts and books about China preach that socializing creates the bond and trust in the relationship; for the Chinese, the everlasting friendship developed over these social activities is worth more than any signed contract one could ever hope for. For MNOs and their executive management, I agree the entertainment activities are a must. The foreign MNOs are depending upon the Chinese government or state-owned company for favorable tax status or entry into a previously closed market or industry. The large state-owned enterprises and government ministries have already preordered the dishes for the banquet, which sometimes take days to prepare. The executives attending are probably old-school traditionalists who still value these social events. These social events have become habit for them, and any cancellation could be viewed as a snub and sign of disrespect.

The situation is quite different for SMBs. I have yet to see a situation in which foreigners were refused business because they declined a dinner invitation or skipped the "bottoms up" drinking competition. The bottom line? Making money. The Chinese will do business with you only if profits are attainable, not because you can sing Frank Sinatra's "My Way" in perfect pitch.

So why do the Chinese continually ask their guests for lunch, and then dinner, and then again for another meal the next day? It's not because they like you or want to get to know you or want to build trust, as suggested by the many China experts. They do so out of habit, like when Westerners unconsciously ask, "How are you?" Westerners are not always particularly interested in their guest's health, nor are the Chinese in many cases particularly interested in dining with their guests, but they ask out of habit and because they think it's just the right thing to do. This goodwill gesture has been around for thousands of years; it's ingrained in the Chinese psyche. My grandmother, regardless of the time of day, would always ask me if I were hungry and would then run into the kitchen and make a couple of Chinese dishes. If I saw her ten times in a day, she would ask me ten times. This was her way of greeting me, and similarly, the way most Chinese businesspeople greet their foreign partners.

All this socializing also serves as a blatant excuse for Chinese managers to eat good food, drink expensive Chinese white wine, and flirt with pretty karaoke girls. It's as simple as that. This especially applies to state-owned enterprises. You see, government companies have large budgets for these sorts of activities, and the managers—actually politicians acting as businesspeople—can't wait to host foreigners for these "important" meetings.

Often when we would go to dinner with them, they would order the most expensive dishes: steamed sea bass, shark-fin soup, or even fresh caviar from France. On top of that, a half-dozen bottles of the most expensive Chinese white wines were usually downed. I always found it funny that even though most foreigners prefer plain old beer to 90-proof Chinese liquor, the Chinese still order it. Why? For themselves, of course. Not only are the meals extravagant, but way too much is usually ordered. This is no accident. Most of the leftover food is doggy-bagged for the managers to take home to their families for a second or even third meal. Lastly, it is telling when you notice the number of people attending these dinners. They usually take up several tables and consist of employees who you have never met and who have absolutely nothing to do with your business. I guess the more the merrier—or maybe the more people, the more freebies.

Be particularly careful when visiting provincial or city-owned enterprises in one of the many secondary or outlier cities where foreigners are less seen. The social activities can be a tool for publicity. On one occasion, I took my American customers to a state-owned factory in Zibou, a city in the northeast region of China. This factory produced rubber stoppers for syringes. We arrived in the late morning and were immediately whisked away to a fancy restaurant and escorted into a large, gaudy private room decorated with fake European antique paintings and furniture. After two hours of eating and drinking (yes, they drank hard liquor at lunch), we were shoved into a minivan and taken to the local Zibou Communist Party office where the Zibou mayor himself greeted us. We sat in typical Communist fashion, with the president and the mayor sitting in chairs in the front and both entourages arranged behind their respected leaders. The local press took pictures and interviewed us for the following day's front-page story, which undoubtedly described all the great deeds the local officials were doing for its citizens. In total, we spent only two hours at the factory, but we had three large, bombastic meals, a half-day tour of the city ruins, and probably ten bottles of Chinese white wine—of which we foreigners drank none. Ultimately, the visit amounted to a big waste of time for my clients, as the factory reeked of so many quality issues that it didn't even make the shortlist.

So, should you socialize? If you plan to do business with a company, then yes, do eat, drink, and sing. Keep in mind, though, you go out not for yourself, but to appease the Chinese partner and to play along with whatever agenda your host may have. And even though it may be a social event, the entertainment is still business. Be sociable, talkative, curious, and most of all, make out like the event was pure fun. Tell your host what a great time you had. However, it's not necessary to overdo the social activities; one dinner and one lunch will adequately fulfill your obligations, and beyond that a polite refusal will suffice.

Conversely, if you have no intention of doing business with a company then save the time and move on. Keep the relationship clean; no one owes the other any favors. Among all the nationalities I have worked with, Americans are the most polite, having difficulty refusing the somewhat pushy invitations from their Chinese hosts. Then after some bonding from a night out, Americans sometimes give in to the hospitality. As gracious as the Chinese can be, tell them politely that you have other matters to attend to, and if they become persistent, the truth is best revealed: let them know that you will have to reconsider the business relationship and explain the reasons why.

Building Trust

Supposedly, the Chinese view trust and personal relationships as an integral part of the business process, and many books about China emphasize that foreigners should be sensitive to and actually reciprocate the same "trusting" feelings. I'm not sure if this trust concept is truly important to the Chinese today (I'll explain later), but either because of habit or a show of hospitality, they certainly act like it's important and want their business partners to think the same. My advice to foreign SMBs: Take the trust factor out of any Chinese business relationship. Be sensitive to it and even go along with it, but never let it be a focal point. You will thank me later for this advice.

I agree that trust was indeed an integral part of doing business in China during the pre-Communist era, when contracts and business laws didn't really exist, thus, forcing businesspeople to rely on trust and personal relationships to do business. I'm sure this was even the case when business laws didn't exist in the West. A simple handshake substituted for contracts. Without any legal recourse, one definitely had to get better insight on their business counterparts, and socializing was the mechanism to do this; it provided a backdrop to analyze, sum up, and draw conclusions about a potential partner. What better way to get to know people then after they've had a few too many drinks or to observe how they handle money than over a game of mahjong.

But things are different today. For one, China does have business laws—though still antiquated and sometimes unenforceable— that allow for some legal recourse. At the very least, an agreement drawn on paper can serve as a reference point when disputes arise. Second, over the past forty years, Communism has virtually wiped out any semblance of trust. The Chinese government—through many years of misdeeds (I'll discuss more about this in future chapters)—has created a society that distrusts its government and officials, public institutions, police force, and especially large corporate companies, private or state-owned. I can comfortably say that the vast majority of Chinese don't really trust anybody outside their immediate family and friends, and I would even question that hypothesis. So if the Chinese have difficulty trusting each other, how will they trust a foreigner whom they just met and have virtually nothing in common with except the desire to make a profit?

Now, I know these comments are troubling. Many have accused me of discrimination or racial profiling. How can I make vast, sweeping generalizations about an ethnicity comprised of 1.3 billion people? I am not describing characteristics that are inherently Chinese. Rather, I am describing the aftermath of a group of people who happen to be Chinese and living in a specific time and place who have gone through a terrifying, life-changing, and tumultuous period known as the Cultural Revolution. Anybody—white, black, or yellow—would have been adversely affected by these catastrophic events. This reign of terror was not just an isolated event that affected a small region within China or a small population; it destroyed a complete generation of Chinese along with their children, and even today their children's children still suffer from the remnants.

If I were making generalizations about the Chinese, then my comments about trust and other issues described later in this book would apply to all Chinese, living in or out of China, before or after the Cultural Revolution. That is not the case. My descriptions apply only to the Chinese who have been affected by Communism from the 1950s to the 1990s. My comments, for example, do not apply to the Chinese living in Taiwan. Though they have similar cultures, languages, and ancestries, in no way would I ever characterize the Taiwanese growing up in the '50s and '60s the same way I would characterize mainland Chinese from the same period. Taiwan was not victimized by Communism, and its citizens lived freely and diversely. Likewise, the younger generation in China today is very different from their forefathers. Their behavior, thinking, and attitudes toward life are much more similar to Westerners, and I would never describe them as I would their parents who lived through this tragedy.

I hope my words, once and for all, squash any inkling that I am a racist, China-hater, or China-basher and that you will allow me to continue on with my sometimes unorthodox—but I believe accurate—descriptions of a generation or two (maybe even three) of Chinese. Unfortunately, these very generations of Chinese are today leading China; they are the current political leaders in the

Communist Party, the current general managers and CEOs of Chinese companies, and the very people who foreign businesspeople will deal with in their day-to-day China activities.

Throughout this book, I will refer to these oppressed victims of Communism as the "Mao Generation" so as to distinguish them from the Chinese who were not affected by the oppression. So again, any description of the Mao Generation is not an attack or generalization of the entire Chinese ethnicity and is isolated to only Chinese who lived in these hellish times. The new Chinese, or as I like to call them the "Me Generation," have almost eerily similar qualities and traits to the thirty-something generation of Westerners and act nothing like their parents. They are educated, well traveled, speak English, and want what every other young person wants in life: a good job, a family, an iPad, and the resources to do what and go where they want—nothing more, nothing less.

Getting back to trust and the Chinese, I have now hopefully succinctly and logically described why many foreign businesspeople are falsely led to believe that trust is an integral part of doing business in China. They go eating, drinking, and singing until the wee hours of the morning and do it again the next day. They talk about their families, their hometowns, and sometimes even the secrets that their spouses don't know about. Suddenly, the foreigners become best friends with their Chinese counterparts and are ready to take the plunge in partnership, abandoning their normally cautious attitudes. Partnerships that begin this way usually end in disaster.

As consultants, we exhibit our services at trade shows, and the people stopping by usually own or work at an SMB. Often the conversations we have with them ultimately lead to solving their China mishaps. I recall an owner of a San Diego plastic kitchenware supplier who shipped over $1 million in steel molds to a Shenzhen contract manufacturer to produce plastic cups, utensils, and plates. The American had a gut feeling about the Chinese factory owner—that he was trustworthy—after spending only two weeks with him.

During that time, the American was invited to the factory owner's summer house in the mountains of Shangdong Province, met his family, enjoyed home cooking made by the owner's eighty-year-old mother, and was lavished with souvenirs and gifts. They played golf together, drank together, and shared the most intimate life stories with each other. They were like brothers. The American was confident that the factory owner was trustworthy to the point that they didn't even draft a contract. He returned home and shipped the molds immediately. To make a long story short, the Shenzhen factory owner closed shop, took the molds, and was never to be seen again.

I asked the American how he could take such a large financial risk without taking standard precautions. "I thought we really trusted each other. No one had ever treated me like that, not even my own brother. I guess I let my emotions run and thought trust was such an important factor for doing business in China. I was wrong, and my gut instincts fooled me." Don't ever follow your gut instincts in China. It will lead to indigestion.

I met a metal alloy parts manufacturer from California who faced a similar predicament. Without proper due diligence and after trusting their Chinese partner in a joint-manufacturing operation in Shanghai, he and his company came to find out that the Chinese partner was actually a fraud. They lacked the licenses to import the specialty equipment, had not registered the new venture properly (resulting in delays and financial penalties), and fell short on financial resources to fund the new venture's operating expenses. The American owner was sucked into believing his Chinese partner after several months of courtship and friendship-bonding events.

The lesson here: don't allow trust to be a deciding factor when choosing to work with a Chinese partner. For sure, Chinese companies will play the trust game—wine and dine you, have you meet the family, play golf with you—but always keep to the business basics. Trust was not one of the business principles I learned in business school, and it was certainly not taught in the Chinese school of hard knocks, at least for the graduating Mao Generation class.

They Say Business Takes Time in China

On the contrary, the pace of business in China moves at light speed, many times faster when compared to the West. The Chinese are in a rush to get rich. They want your purchase orders quickly. They want your products shipped right away. They want to make money before some intervening force—market conditions, the government, or the police—impedes their stop-at-nothing mission. I have witnessed intricate steel molds made in a week that would have taken months in the States, examined prototype medical products crafted by hand only days after the manufacturer received the drawings, and signed contracts after just a few hours of negotiations. The pace of business in China is like no other I have seen in other countries.

Business takes time in China only for foreigners. Translation will easily double or triple the conversation time. Cultural differences can spur misunderstandings, lengthening business dealings by weeks if not months. And time differences turn simple, mundane tasks—waiting for e-mail replies, setting up conference calls, sending samples—into complicated, painful, laborious tests of one's patience. On top of that, foreigners sometimes treat their China business as an "out of sight, out of mind" hobby, one in which they are only engaged when in China. Back at home, they tend to other important matters, and thus ignore and delay their Chinese business even further.

The Chinese Lack Creativity?

When foreign MNOs first set foot in China in the late 1980s and early '90s, they found the local staff—managers, engineers, and salesmen—to be stiff in their thinking and creativity. Engineers exhibited excellent technical skills and accountants demonstrated great bookkeeping expertise; they knew their trade well but had no ability to apply what they learned to new and different situations. Further, local professionals only did what their foreign management told them to do—nothing more, nothing less. They lacked the creativity to come up with new ideas. They acted on command without questioning or analyzing if the orders were really the correct way to go about things.

This was frustrating for foreign managers who were accustomed to give-and-take discussions in the decision-making process. Plus, they knew nothing about doing business in China and were seeking feedback from the locals. They received almost none; everybody acted like robots.

This brain freeze was partially due to Communism. Chairman Mao wanted his people simply to obey and do as they were told. Anybody thinking differently was thought to be infected with Western propaganda and was sent out to the countryside for reeducation. You had to act and think a certain way; anything different created attention and would probably earn you a visit by the infamous Red Guards for a good beating. Big Brother indeed was watching you. You were banned from making money, could not travel, were ostracized for wearing non-Maoist clothing, and were tortured for reading scholarly books. Everybody was poor, or as the Communists put it, everybody was treated equally—except for government officials, who were considered more equal than others.

Communist China adopted the Russian educational system; students memorized, mimicked, and repeated what they were taught. Free thinking was not allowed. Professors taught students only what to do and how to do it, not giving them any free rein to think "beyond the box." They were to just do as they were told. Engineers, for example, were taught physics and mathematics but could not apply the lessons to solve new problems, invent products, or come up with new scientific discoveries.

Upon graduation, students were sent to work at the SOEs, where any remaining remnants of creativity were stamped to death by boredom and indifference. There was no incentive to work hard since these antiquated, money-losing government shops, mostly factories, served basically as welfare houses whose sole purpose was to keep as many people employed as possible. I remember in 1987 when I visited a television transformer factory outside of Shanghai, I literally saw five people standing under a ladder changing a lightbulb. People were sleeping on the office floors, and assembly lines were overcrowded with operators; some did nothing while two or three others performed the work of one person.

Before Communism, China for centuries had been a hotbed for inventions and creative thinking. Christopher Wright, Australian government's senior trade commissioner based in Shanghai, explained, "I only need to say four words about this issue: Gunpowder. Printing press. Paper. Compass. All have been invented by the Chinese. They invented the H-bomb from the A-bomb faster than any other nation. There's nothing wrong with Chinese creativity—it's a misconception."

My favorite example of Chinese ingenuity was the ability of Chinese sailors in 1433 to transport a full-grown, living giraffe from Kenya to China, covering some six thousand miles on a large wooden sailing ship.[1] This was not just done once, but at least four other times. Imagine the intricacies involved in moving a twenty-foot animal weighing about sixteen hundred pounds on a boat, and at the same time, having to keep it alive for several months.

Chinese creativity, ingenuity, and entrepreneurship are on the rise once again. The Me Generation, now in their twenties and thirties, work in profit-driven companies, speak fluent English, watch Western television shows, and regularly travel abroad. Their creative juices are pouring as they strive to become rich, promoted, or famous. Young businesspeople, engineers, and scientists work at foreign companies to learn the newest technologies, associate with world-class leaders, and strive to better themselves economically.

---

[1] Louise Levathes, *When China Ruled the Seas: The Treasure Fleet of the Dragon Throne, 1405–1433* (New York: Oxford University Press, 1996), 172–73.

In the past, products were only manufactured and copied in China. Today, they are designed and developed in China. In the future, they will be invented and discovered in China. This can be witnessed by all the MNOs initiating engineering and design centers throughout China. Companies like Intel, IBM, Tyco, Siemens, and Alcatel-Lucent are all inventing and designing technologies in China with highly educated and creative Chinese engineers and scientists. Similarly, before the MNOs had their China advertising and marketing campaigns produced by their headquarters or farmed out to one of the New York agencies. Today, Chinese locals, just as creative and daring as New York's best, design and produce the local commercials, print ads, and catchphrases. And soon, if not already, they will produce campaigns for Europe and the United States.

Communism aside, cultural differences have also added to the creativity misconception. Westerners associate silence with timidity, lackluster thinking, and unresponsiveness. For the Chinese, it's a sign of humility and respect for authority. In pre-Communist China, Confucianism, the de facto religion, taught children to respect their parents, students to respect their teachers, and government ministers to respect their emperor. Subordinates were expected to behave a certain way, and talking back, disagreeing, or voicing a different opinion was shunned or frowned upon.

I recall one incident from when I was working at Philips Lighting's Shanghai electronic ballast factory in 1994. I had been given the task of developing a new electronic ballast for China; the current product, from Europe, was overpriced, overspecified, and simply too "European" for China. Not knowing the local market, I summoned staff from various departments—engineering, sales, and marketing—to have an all-day brainstorming session. Well, the all-day meeting was short—about thirty minutes. I asked questions, shot out ideas, but nobody budged. Complete silence. Later, I asked one of the engineers why no one spoke out. He told me that they felt uncomfortable voicing their opinions among their peers, especially directly to a vice president. It just wasn't right to be telling a senior manager how to do things.

Does Group Harmony Trump Individualism?

One of Mao Zedong's goals during the Cultural Revolution was to wipe out any elements that were deemed counterrevolutionary or viewed as a credible threat to his authoritarian dictatorship. This included the destruction of religious sites and historical relics, the burning of books, the defamation of Western values and cultures, and, probably the most the destructive of all, the separation of family members—children from mother, wife from husband. Mao replaced traditional family teachings and values associated with respect, trust, compassion, and honesty with his *Little Red Book*, which contained the teachings and moral lessons that Mao and the Communist Party wanted to instill in the population. Men and women forming a group called the Red Guards were the self-declared enforcers of Mao's teachings; truly, they were just a bunch of hooligans who tortured and murdered anybody they thought was against the Communist Party.

The Cultural Revolution also wiped out Confucianism's teachings and its emphasis on group harmony, education, respect for elders, and honesty. Children were actually taught to distrust their parents and even report subversive or antigovernment activities occurring in their families. They grew up distrusting their own families, living under a corrupt government, and surviving only by their own cunning and prowess.

So where does this leave us today? We are left with a Mao Generation with little or no moral compass. Group harmony is the last thing on a Chinese businessperson's mind. Oh sure, on the surface they preach the themes of promoting friendship, win-win business, and cooperation. But on the inside, it's just a dog-eat-dog world for them. They grew up in a world of corruption, bribery, nepotism, and money laundering and can't change suddenly just because the government commands them to become model citizens. And unfortunately, most of our business dealings are with Mao Generation Chinese, ranging from ages forty to seventy something.

In the Chinese government itself, Chinese Prime Minister Wen Jiabao and past president Jiang Zemin both acknowledge corruption as the number-one problem affecting China's worldwide business standing and its current inability to implement laws and policies.[2] In just the past few years we have witnessed horrendous acts of corruption, such as milk companies adding toxic chemicals to the milk supply and accusations that government officials were skimming school construction money, which led to hundreds of children dying under crumbling schools in the aftermath of the 2008 Chengdu earthquakes. On a smaller scale, I personally have seen dozens of acts of corruption. Some are nickel-and-dime acts: lower-grade steel used in syringe needles, pirated business software, or unpaid wire transfers. Other instances, however, are mind-boggling: exporting hormone- and pesticide-contaminated

---

2 Ted Plafker, *Doing Business in China* (New York: Hachette Book Group USA, 2008), 239.

fish, knowingly selling defective baby car seats, and installing faulty electronics used in emergency medical systems.

Foreign SMBs particularly must be careful, since they are more likely to deal with Chinese business owners who are acting on their own without having corporate oversight or governance. It is imperative that foreign businesspeople seek alternative ways, other than trust or contracts, to prove, substantiate, and confirm their business dealings. I discuss these methods in later chapters.

On a positive note, the Me Generation—the under-forty age group—is nothing like the older Mao Generation. They are more like you and me, having Western ethical and moral values. They want to do business the right way. I see signs of this every day. For example, on one automotive parts project, a young Chinese engineering manager called me about a shipment. He informed me that the metal used for a transmission part was not in line with specifications, and that they would send replacement parts immediately. The Chinese manager wouldn't have had to do this, since my customer probably would have never known.

Intellectual Property Theft: It's Not the Culture

China business experts often blame China's lack of intellectual property rights (IPR) protection on culture and history. They write that Confucianism emphasizes the sharing of knowledge and information and that truth should not be owned by individuals or any one institution. Based on this logic we are led to believe that the pirating of DVDs and CDs and the selling of Nike and Chanel knockoffs are deeply embedded in the Chinese culture, and thus the Chinese should be excused for these blatantly illegal acts. I'm sorry, but I don't buy this one bit. First, the experts are making a stretch when comparing knowledge and truth to DVDs and tennis shoes. I'm no Confucius expert, but I think he meant all individuals had an inherent right to learn, so education should be free and not a paid endeavor; subjects like physics or mathematics are universal to everyone and not owned by private institutions. He did not mean that humankind has the inalienable right to watch Indiana Jones movies for free. Second, Confucian philosophy also taught the "rule of man," and man has clearly stated that intellectual property rights are to be protected, even in China. Confucius would not teach his followers to disobey their country's laws.

China's lack of IPR protection is due to the central government's lackadaisical attitude toward the enforcement of the IPR laws that already exist on the books. Basically, they have more pressing matters at hand: providing work to the masses, a worldwide economic downturn that has closed thousands of factories and slashed China's 2009 GDP by half, and supplying sufficient raw materials—oil, concrete, and copper—to spur their rapid growth.

When President Obama made his first visit to China in 2009, Beijing suddenly made IPR a priority, or at least on a temporary basis. We saw videos of police cracking down on DVD factories and raiding offices that were using pirated Microsoft Office software. These made-for-television scenes were more for public relations than for any real, long-term results. Obama left, and the fake DVDs were back on the streets the next day.

Another reason for the lack of enforcement is simply that protecting IPR serves no self-interest for the central government at this time. Chinese companies are not producing their own IP and thus couldn't care less whether the intellectual property rights of MNOs are being infringed upon. Indeed, this attitude will change as Chinese companies design and invent technologies and products and make movies for international release. IPR enforcement typically occurs at the local level, and the smaller cities actually see these IPR crackdowns as a negative to their local economies. Local companies and factories, even those producing fake DVDs and Chanel knockoffs, provide jobs and pay taxes (sometimes). The economic downturn will bring millions of job losses and factory closings, so I anticipate seeing little change in China's IPR policies, at least for a few more years.

Chapter 1 Summary

1. Don't be fooled by all the hocus-pocus that consultants or books about China teach foreigners about doing business in China. It's just a bunch of gimmicks used to make money or make foreigners think China is so vastly different from the West. Indeed, China is different. It has its small quirks and variations, but in the end, you still need to apply the same basic business principles to China that made you successful in your home country.

2. Guanxi used to be important in China when money, goods, and resources were scarce. But things are different today, and guanxi doesn't play any more significant a role than relationships or connections do in the West. You don't need guanxi to be successful in China.

3. China experts are always telling foreigners that "saving face" or mianzi is extremely important in China. Indeed, you should be sensitive to this but not to the point that it takes you out of your normal business conduct and behavior. Ultimately, just be yourself. If you must say something that may lose mianzi for your Chinese counterpart, then so be it.

4. Drinking and socializing with the Chinese will not make or break a business deal. It won't turn a bad deal into a better one. The Chinese don't necessarily want to socialize with you either. They do it out of habit, like when foreigners ask "How are you?" We don't really care about the response; it's just asked out of courtesy.

5. Chinese businesspeople seemingly want to build a trusting relationship with you. They take you to dinner, lavish you with gifts, and guide you on sightseeing excursions. Don't be fooled by these antics. Trust should never be a deciding factor when doing business in China. Members of the Mao Generation, the generation that suffered the most during the Cultural Revolution, have little concept of trust and are simply looking out for themselves.

6. Contrary to what many foreigners believe, business moves at the speed of light in China. The Chinese are in a rush to make money fast. So many things can change in a matter of weeks—laws, politics, exchange rates, economic policies—that may take months or years in the West, so it's imperative to make money now.

7. China is one of the most creative societies in the world. After all, the Chinese invented papermaking, the compass, gunpowder, and printing. The Cultural Revolution thwarted creativity, as Mao wanted people to be subservient to his teachings and twisted ideologies. But today's generation, the Me Generation, are just as creative and innovative as the best engineers, scientists, and businesspeople in the West.

8. Foreigners are often misled to believe that the Chinese are group oriented, choosing group harmony over individualism. Nothing could be further from the truth. The Cultural Revolution destroyed all family values and Confucianism that taught respect for elders and the belief that the whole takes precedence over the individual.

Chapter 2
Finding Your Chinese Partner

Whether an SMB plans to sell services and products into China or outsource from China, a local partner—distributor, manufacturer, agent, or representative—must be found. It is almost impossible to do things on your own during the initial entry phases. Finding this trusted partner is a difficult task when the culture, language, and business climates are unknown quantities. Americans, in particular when compared to Europeans, have unique issues when developing trust with the Chinese. I find Americans overly trusting and too eager to befriend their Chinese partners. As a Chinese American, I myself fall into the same trap. When I first meet people, I want to trust them and believe their words and ostensible sincerity. In return I hope this goodwill will be reciprocated and that my potential partner will believe and trust me. We want to like our business partners, and we want to be liked. This, however, can often lead to big trouble.

Most Americans have higher standards of living relative to the rest of the world. We may have a place to live, a good education, a decent-paying job, and discretionary income to afford traveling, eating out, and nice clothes. Because of this good life, we perceive the world differently—some say through rose-colored glasses. And thus, we view people differently. For the most part, people have been good to us, and we are good to others.

For centuries, Chinese history, culture, and folktales taught virtue, morality, and kindness. Famous philosophers like Confucius and Laozi dedicated their lives to writing and pondering the essences of integrity, truth, trust, respect, and consideration for others. I have experienced many acts of kindness while working and living in China—being invited to strangers' homes for dinner or escorted to my destination when lost. However, trust in China is not what it was like in the pre-Mao era. Communism, the Cultural Revolution, and the Great Leap Forward broke down Chinese traditional values. Today, making money, at any cost, has taken a priority for many, especially for the Mao Generation. And this lack of integrity perpetuates throughout all of China, to the point that the government has it listed as one of the top ten social diseases in the country. Thus, we have the present situation: counterfeit products, intellectual property infringement, tainted medicines, government bribery, fake powdered milk for babies, and widespread labor abuses. Fortunately, as the Chinese have begun reflecting more and more on their past, Confucianism is now allowed and is making a comeback. Traditional moral values are reemerging, although in many respects there is still a long way to go.

On top of the historic erosion of traditional Chinese values, business dealings worth thousands of times the average middle manager's annual salary further the temptation to cheat. Americans come to me amazed as to why a company or Chinese businessperson would throw away a good business deal worth maybe several hundred thousand dollars for just a few thousand dollars. China is still a poor country, with an annual per capita income of $2,900 compared to $39,000[3] in the United States.[4] The disparity further widens in the countryside, where 70 percent of China's population still live, earning just under $900 per year.[5] You can now see how a Chinese businessperson might consider it well worth it to risk his or her life for a few thousand dollars. Most have never seen that amount of cash. The lesson to be learned is this: we cannot use our own reference point to measure trust or how the Chinese will behave because we come from such different economic, social, and moral backgrounds.

The Underground Economy

China's underground economy is worth billions of dollars as estimated by many economists.[6] This black market includes counterfeit consumer products, intellectual property theft, tax evasion, and unlicensed factories and businesses operating under the noses of corrupt city officials. Exact figures are impossible to calculate, but I imagine this could amount to 20 to 30 percent of China's actual economy.

Twenty years ago, the tricks were simple and easy to figure out, since the Chinese were just out for nickels and dimes. I recall in the early nineties when I would receive a phone call, like clockwork,

3 news.xinhuanet.com, "China Urban Residents per Capita Income Grows 7.8% in 2010," January 20, 2011.

4 *Survey of Current Business* (US Department of Commerce, Bureau of Economic Analysis), 2011.

5 news.xinhuanet.com, "China Urban Residents per Capital Income Grows 7.8% in 2010," January 20, 2011.

6 Shaun Rein, Forbes.com, "No, China Will Absolutely Not Collapse," February 3, 2010.

upon checking into my hotel room in Shanghai or Beijing. The caller was always a man pretending to ask for someone else. After apologizing and some small talk, the conversation would lead to whether I would be interested in buying some rare Chinese antiques or traditional Chinese medicines like bear paws and tiger penises. I never took the bait, but many of my colleagues did. In the end, no real harm was done, and we all got a good laugh, only losing a few hundred dollars in the process.

The game is different today. Black marketers are looking for hundreds of thousands—if not millions—of dollars, and they are willing to risk their lives for it. In late 2009, I received a purchase order for one of my customers, a Korean water purifier manufacturer. The order was for several thousand units, worth over $5 million. I was dumbfounded, as I'd been trying to market and sell these Korean purifiers for two years without receiving a single order. How could I suddenly receive an order from this company when I had never even met a single one of their employees? They didn't even negotiate prices, and most Chinese people will haggle over anything for any amount, from a $10 fake Rolex watch to a Caterpillar tractor costing $200,000. The company's only request was for a salesperson to visit the headquarters located an hour away from Lanzhou, a city in western China not known for commercial business. I was excited but suspicious at the same time, as it sounded too good to be true. I knew a more thorough investigation was needed.

Phone calls to the company revealed nothing out of the ordinary. To prove they had funds, I asked for bank drafts. No problems there. I inquired about their business model. They said they had a monopoly on the area's water-related businesses, having close ties with the provincial government and SOEs. I still felt something was not right, but who was I to look a gift horse in the mouth? I was ready to go.

I called my mother just to say hello the day before my trip to Lanzhou. She sarcastically warned me not to get kidnapped there. As it turned out, that region was known for kidnapping foreign businesspeople and holding them for ransom. The kidnappers specifically went after smaller companies, not wanting to create an international crisis. After ransom demands for sums between $5,000 and $20,000, most foreign companies simply succumbed and handed over the small amounts in hopes of getting their employees back safely. Needless to say, I postponed my Lanzhou trip. Thanks, Mom.

Taking the Trust Factor Out

On average I take about ten calls a month from individuals or SMBs asking me to solve their China-related problems. SMBs go to China on their own, thinking they are well versed in Chinese business skills given their international experience in such countries as Canada, France, or Brazil. But just how different China is from the rest of the world comes as a complete surprise. The SMBs come from various industries and have diverse problems, but 60 to 80 percent of the root causes of their problems fall into the same class: they were too trusting of their Chinese business counterparts.

This story of one such company illustrates my point: A large bicycle distributor from Florida was having trouble getting bicycles from a Chinese factory. The owner, John, had found this factory through the famous China outsourcing website Alibaba. com. After sending messages to several factories, a Shanghai factory quickly returned his e-mails, and thus began two weeks of communications and negotiations. Without visiting the factory, or even having a conversation over the phone, John wired $200,000 for container loads of bicycles, tricycles, and spare parts.

The factory promised shipment within sixty days after receipt of payment. Well, sixty days came and went. E-mails again went back and forth, and the company promised the shipment would leave China within sixty days. After nine months John received half his order, but felt he was getting empty promises for the remaining balance. He called me and asked for assistance.

My immediate question to John was, "How in the world could you send that kind of money to an overseas company without at least having a conversation with them?" His reply, "I've been doing business with European and South American companies for many years and never had problems like this. We wired hundreds of thousands of dollars in the past without needing to visit them. Business was like clockwork—we wired the money, and the product came ninety days later."

Welcome to China, John. I lectured John for several minutes and then proceeded to try to solve his problems. For me this case was unusual in that the factory had at least honored half of the order. If the owners had been out to cheat John, they would have simply disappeared. Further, John was still getting e-mails from the factory—though they were untrue—promising that the remaining products would ship soon.

John wired the funds in September of 2008. This was in the midst of the world financial crisis and the AIG, Lehman Brothers, and Merrill Lynch debacles. China, too, was struggling with a massive downturn in exports, especially in the toy industry. Thousands of toy and toy-related factories were closing in China as the big American toy companies like Hasbro and Mattel were canceling orders. I suspected the same fate for this bicycle company.

At John's request I made a surprise visit to the factory, and as expected, saw a dilapidated building that looked almost abandoned. Broken bicycles, tricycles, and wooden crates were scattered about as children played hide and seek in the wreckage. I eventually made contact with the owner. I must admit that I expected to meet a typical Mao Generation businessperson: a man from the countryside, maybe in his fifties, who had graduated from the school of hard knocks and had little remorse for his misdeeds. I was wrong this time.

He was in no way a deceitful man and had never had any bad intentions. Rather, he had just fallen on bad times with the sudden economic downturn. He had used half of John's money for actual production and the remainder to pay back debts. It was still his plan to finish the order as soon as he could borrow the funds to open up the factory again.

On another assignment, I negotiated the licensing fees owed to a California software developer who licensed its software to a computer distributor in Shenzhen. The Chinese company owed approximately $40,000. When asked why they did not want to pay, the owner screamed back, "Why should I pay them when they are making millions and we are a small, struggling company? We opened the China market for them, and they show no gratitude for this. It's fair we keep our share of the money." Finding common ground can be difficult when the counterpart uses this sort of logic. However, this is often the mentality of the Mao Generation, who have been too poor for too long. They want payback now and have an "it's my turn to get rich" attitude.

My relatives living in China had a similar outlook on money and life. In 1988 I accompanied my father to Shenyang, a city in northeastern China, where he was teaching a summer course at Northeast University. This was my first trip to China and my father's first trip since he fled from China to Taiwan in 1949. Most of my father's relatives fled to Taiwan, except for his third sister; she decided to stay in Wuhan with her husband and children. Not having seen his sister for almost forty years, he invited her to Shenyang. My father was very excited; it would be wonderful to catch up with his long-lost sister.

The first couple of hours went well; both had much to say and ask. But soon after, things started going sour. She talked about how life had been difficult during the Cultural Revolution. Her son was currently unemployed, and her granddaughter was having health problems. My father offered to help. The next day, she presented him with a wish list: a refrigerator, a television, a washer, a dryer, money for her granddaughter's education, a monthly stipend for her son's living expenses, money to repair her husband's gravesite, and on and on. As she described each item, her tone was not of sincerity or gratitude, but rather of disdain, hatred, and jealousy. She had suffered so much, and now it was her turn to reap the rewards that others had (metaphorically speaking) taken away from her. These monies were owed to her, and it was payback time. My father was a symbol of all she didn't have, of what could have become of her and her family. She was bitter and full of resentment for what Communism had done to her.

Contempt is a common trait of the Mao Generation. After they've cheated someone, they tell me that in fact they are actually the victims and the foreign companies are the perpetrators. I sometimes don't even know how to start the discussion as we are so far apart on our positions. Somehow, someway, they think we are to blame for the dark days of the Cultural Revolution and their bad luck.

Don't Trust Your Gut Instincts

As much as I preach to my clients to take the trust factor out in China, foreign businesspeople still cannot steer away from it. Foreigners may accept my advice for the "hard" issues like contracts, negotiation methods, and payment terms without questioning my experience or expertise. The "soft" issues, however—trust and relationship building—are a different story. Americans want to use their gut instincts to judge whether their counterparts are trustworthy enough to partner with.

I recall a gut decision that backfired for one of my clients. We found a syringe factory in Wenzhou, along the east coast of China, for a Minnesota-based medical disposable supplier. We visited the factory four times in nine months for various inspections and supplier audits. During these trips, the American vice president of quality, Patrick, became good acquaintances with the factory owner, going out for dinners and karaoke regularly. I had my doubts about the owner; he was a Mao Generation baby and a self-made millionaire. As I wrote about in chapter 1, these Mao children went through hell. They lived their younger days suspicious of their own families, trusting no one except themselves and their own survival instincts.

As we negotiated the quality specifications, I recommended to Patrick that we hire local manufacturing engineers to oversee the first several months of production and then ease off the inspections as we observed more consistent quality. On one of our earlier trips, we noticed many quality inconsistencies: unlabeled bags containing syringes, water leaking into clean-air rooms, and an excessive amount of poor-quality Chinese-made resin, which is usually used for toy manufacturing and not for higher-quality medical products. We were afraid these cheaper materials would be substituted for the higher-quality Japanese-made resin we had specified in the contract. We also questioned how this factory could quote syringe prices 30 percent lower than the next-lowest bidder and still use high-quality materials and maintain stringent inspection standards.

Of course, the added personnel would increase costs, which bothered Patrick. On top of that, Patrick told me that he had full confidence in the owner. "Listen, Stanley," he said. "I know people very well, and I now know Li Zhong [the factory owner] like the back of my hand. You see the real person after a few bottles of whiskey. I should know, I have over forty years' experience; Li Zhong will be good to us and good to me—he gave me his personal guarantee."

Who was I to argue with Patrick, a man with over forty years of experience inspecting and auditing factories all over the world? Was I to tell him that his experience in Europe or Mexico had little relation to the present situation in China? No, not me. A sixty-two-year-old man with his experience can definitely read into people better than a forty-year-old MBA engineering geek. Patrick was my customer, and I could only push so far. After all, the customer is always right. Right?

Production started off well. This is typical for many Mao Generation–owned factories; the initial batches, or golden samples, are always perfect because the Chinese know that the first several months' products are intensely scrutinized. Unfortunately, but not unexpectedly for me, we found problems after twelve months. The resin was not the specified material from Japan, the steel for the needles was not from Germany, and many of the measured quality parameters did not conform to the contracted specifications.

My client lost time and money on this failed project, but the worst part was that it all could have been avoided if we had simply implemented some safety measures along the supply chain. Even with added costs, my client still would have profited handsomely, saving 40 percent over European suppliers. I tried many times to persuade the company to go to China again, but the president would have no more of China, fearing that all factories were cheaters.

I have a closet full of gut-call failures. Older businesspeople in their fifties and sixties tend to fall prey to these mistakes, as do more Americans than Europeans. I can only guess that more senior managers rely more on instincts than facts, and that Americans have less international experience than Europeans, who benefit from their close proximity to the Eastern bloc countries. The lesson here: trust, personal relationships, and personal guarantees are never to replace ironclad proof.

If You Must Trust, Then Whom?

Even after all this hoopla about advising SMBs to take out the trust factor, businesspeople will still retreat to old habits, making decisions based on whether they trust their business counterparts. Believe me, I have lectured dozens of executives to avoid this "soft" approach when choosing a partner, but in the end, they still prefer the old-fashioned way: looking into the eyes of their Chinese partner and making that instinctive judgment about whether they can be entrusted to make baby food, medical IV bags, or toys.

So if my clients must go on intuition, I have outlined a method (shown in chart 2.1) for the best way to do that, though I admit it is not foolproof. Again, I do not necessarily condone using this chart; rather, I developed it as a last resort since my clients continue to ask, "Would you do business with this guy? Can you trust him?"

Chart 2.1 Trusting Individuals

Degree of Trust	More Trustworthy	Less Trustworthy
Education Level	Trade school, college degree, or higher	No more than a high school education
Education Location	Foreign country	China
Financial Background	Wealthier	Poorer
Work Experience	1) International 2) Foreign companies 3) Larger corporations 4) Public companies	1) Only in China 2) Domestic companies 3) SMBs 4) Private companies
Hometown	Major city	Countryside or secondary city
English/Foreign Language	Yes	No
Work Tenure	Three to five years with each company	Short stints at many companies
Industry Tenure	Many years in one industry	Changing industries regularly
Age	Under thirty-five years old	Over fifty years old

Education Level
It's not that uneducated people are inherently more unethical or less trustworthy than educated ones, rather it's expected that college graduates have had formal schooling on morality and ethics and thus will know the difference between right and wrong.

They may still, in the end, choose to do something illegal, but at least it was a conscious decision to do so. May uneducated Chinese, or any ethnicity for that matter, actually don't realize what they are doing is illegal or life-threatening. As the saying goes, "Ignorance is bliss."

Take the Mattel toy example I brought up in the introduction. I spoke to an owner at one of the toy factories accused of using lead paint. He explained to me, "We feel very bad about the lead paint incident, but we never knew lead could harm children. No one explained to us that lead was dangerous. We are not murderers like the foreign companies say we are—we just didn't know."

Insiders at Mattel claim the use of lead paint was strictly forbidden and clearly written in all supplier-related contracts, so ignorance is not an excuse. Many factory owners are uneducated, and thus lack the knowledge and sophistication to read a hundred-page vendor contract. They consider it a waste of money to hire a lawyer. As long as they know the most basic terms—price, delivery dates, specifications, and most important, profit margins—owners will sign almost anything.

Similarly, if a Chinese national has international work experience or has worked in a large foreign subsidiary in China, the person undoubtedly knows what is expected in terms of business behavior. The large multinationals—IBM, Motorola, Nestle—put their local staff through human resources and business-conduct training, similar to what parent companies do in the United States. This international work experience also allows locals to learn and speak English, socialize and interact with foreigners, and experience Western culture. These Chinese are easy to spot in a crowd: they typically present and dress themselves more professionally, use English slang or jargon, and love talking about their overseas experience with foreigners.

Where Are You From?

In China, it's customary to judge a fellow countryperson's personality or physical qualities according to their hometown. Chinese from the northeast are characterized as taller than most Chinese, with more striking facial features, while southerners are thought to be shorter with flatter or softer facial features. The more interesting stereotypes are the personality characterizations. Northeasterners are known to be aggressive, hot-tempered, and sometimes physically violent, while Shanghainese are regarded as intelligent, shrewd in business, and calculating. Some Chinese take these stereotypes very seriously and will not do business with northeasterners; however, the vast majority do not ascribe much truth to these generalizations, and they serve more as the basis for lighthearted sarcasm among friends and business associates.

My mother was an exception; she took these stereotypes very seriously. Growing up, she was taught to never associate with northeastern Chinese. They were the crudest among all the Chinese, lacking in manners, taste, and sophistication. Unfortunately for her, she married my father, who was from Shenyang, a city in northeastern China, but she didn't find that out until twenty years after they were married. On their first date my father lied about his lineage, saying he was from Tianjin. After he confessed the truth twenty years later, my mother didn't speak to him for a month.

For foreigners, however, just having a general idea of where your Chinese counterpart comes from—city or countryside—can reveal valuable information, specifically their financial and family background. People originating from the countryside are among the poorest in China. Today, over 99 percent of China's poor live in or come from rural areas. Most are farmers who live in dilapidated houses with no windows or plumbing, having to use ditches or makeshift outhouses as toilets. They live off the land, farming vegetables and tending to a small number of farm animals. Anything extra is sold or bartered off. Realizing no future, many of the younger generation migrate to cities like Shenzhen or Wenzhou in search of factory work. Luckier ones, using their family's savings, are able to obtain a university education or learn a trade like electronics or engine repair. Most of today's factory owners come from the countryside and have heartwarming "rags to riches" stories, some almost unbelievable.

I stand a little more on guard when dealing with countryside business owners. It's not that countryside folks are inherently bad, but most lack the education, worldly knowledge, and experience to understand what foreign businesspeople expect of them. Some owners are just plain bad, whether they came from the city or countryside or are college-educated or not. But others, because of their rural background, simply don't know what is right and what is wrong. Many mishaps can be avoided if you know who you are dealing with.

City folks, on the other hand, grew up in richer, more Westernized environments. Since market reforms in the late 1970s, China's central government put all its efforts into building, investing in, and promoting major cities. City dwellers on average have better access to health care, job opportunities, and education, and they enjoy higher per capita incomes—over three times those of people in rural areas. Most urban dwellers grew up with a television, telephone, and refrigerator in their apartment, were educated at least through high school, and now even have spending money to travel abroad. These urban Chinese look, feel, and act more like Westerners, and in turn, know what is expected of them when dealing with foreign businesspeople.

Multiple Industries Means Trouble

Chinese businesspeople who cheat and swindle to make a living cannot stay in one industry or location for long. Their history will soon catch up to them, and eventually nobody will associate with them, forcing them to seek refuge in a new town and search for a new business and, unfortunately, a new scam. This is why I become weary when I see an entrepreneur with a history of owning multiple companies in multiple locations in multiple industries. Likewise, an employee having many short employment stints in many locations signals a potential red flag.

I recall one visit to a syringe factory in Yangzhou, about four hours by car northwest of Shanghai. The owner, Mr. Yang, picked us up at our hotel in his chauffeured M-Class Mercedes, wearing the latest Armani suit. On the way to the factory Mr. Yang proudly told me he had owned and sold four businesses in the past ten years. Each of the businesses had been in totally different industries and locations—syringes in Yangzhou, scrap metal in Shenzhen, paper products in Wuhan, and motorcycle engines in Jinan.

Suspicious of Mr. Yang but not having any real evidence, I told my American buyers to keep their eyes and ears open for anything out of the ordinary during our factory tour. Sure enough, we picked up on several discrepancies: new, never-used plastic-injection molding machines, line workers smoking in a clean-air room, and many months' worth of inventory piled up in the warehouses. The factory was five years old, so why the new equipment? Why so much finished goods inventory? Mr. Yang and his team could not give us any plausible answers. I admit each of these minor setbacks alone would not be enough to discredit the owner, but when combined as a whole and with the distinct possibility that Mr. Yang was a fraud, doing business with them was not worth the risk.

Age

As you know by now, I classify Chinese businesspeople into two age groups: those who suffered through the Cultural Revolution, and those who didn't. It's that simple. Those under forty years of age, the Me Generation, experienced little or no impact from the reign of terror, having grown-up in the 1980s and '90s, the beginning stages of China's market-reform campaigns. They lived in relatively normal times and conditions. This generation grew up with a strong family base: mother, father, and grandparents and cousins, sometimes all under one roof. Inklings of Confucian teachings and traditional Chinese values came back, so they know right from wrong and good from evil.

It's the seniors or the Mao Generation, the ones over fifty years old, whom I worry about the most. They grew up alone, living in fear of their own families. Today, many remain bitter and seek refuge or revenge for that lost time. Lacking morality, this generation is capable of doing just about anything for personal advancement, and we have witnessed as much— tainted baby formula, poisoned pet food, and pesticide-laced mushrooms, all of which were caused by individuals from the Mao Generation.

Throughout my business dealings, I have had opportunities to speak with many of these older folks who lived through the Cultural Revolution. Sixty-five-year-old Shenzhen business owner Li Jung said, "I was incarcerated for many years in the countryside. It was the worst time of my life. They took away my youth, my passion to live, and my family. Even today, I live the memories every day. I try to go about my daily life as if nothing happened, but it's hard, very hard."

We are dealing with a generation of older Chinese—business owners, executives, and government leaders—who have essentially lived in an asylum for half their lives. After years of torment, torture, and brainwashing, they were let go into society to try to restart their lives. It's almost impossible; there must be lingering effects: feelings of hatred or resentment, or the desire for revenge. Let me put it another way: I would be concerned if my business associate had been locked up in a mental hospital for over twenty years and then one day, suddenly, was let back into society. This is essentially what happened to the Mao Generation.

Selecting Chinese Companies

Chart 2.2 outlines some criteria I use to assess the viability and trustworthiness of Chinese companies. Again, it is not meant to be a foolproof method, and certainly other decision factors— experience, technical skills, sales, marketing, along with many others—should go into the final decision process.

Chart 2.2 Trusting Companies

Degree of Trust	More Trustworthy	Neutral	Less Trustworthy
Company Ownership	1) Foreign subsidiaries 2) Foreign joint ventures	1) State-owned enterprises (SOEs) 2) Subsidiaries of SOEs 3) Domestic public companies	SMBs with fewer than fifty employees
Industry-Specific	Strong government control: banking, medical, oil and gas, telecommunications, automotive	Moderate government control: agriculture, textiles, foods	Little government control: low-tech manufacturing, toys, consumer electronics, components
Management	Many foreigners involved in day-to-day activities	Western-educated Chinese	Chinese with no international experience
Overseas Sales	More than 50%	20 to 30%	Less than 10%
Company Location	Major cities	Secondary cities	Small cities and towns
Management and Employee Makeup	More than 50% from same city as company	20-30% from same city as company	Less than 10% from same city as company
Employee Morale	High	Average	Low
Customer Base	Large corporations	Medium-size corporations	Consumers
International Sales	Western Europe, United States	South America	Eastern Europe, Africa
Company Physical Appearance	1) Large equipment installed 2) Many employees 3) Office appears busy	1) In present location for at least two years	1) Simple offices (easy to move) 2) Few employees 3) Inactivity

Government-Controlled Industries

In general, more tightly controlled industries are apt to be more trustworthy. Take the medical industry; they have strict government guidelines on registration, exporting, and accounting and are subject to government quality and safety inspections. The central government highly regulates this sector, as it wants to be a worldwide leader in the medical and pharmaceutical industries. The government has poured billions of dollars into medical research development and high-tech medical parks, and it has attracted the world's finest pharmaceutical and medical companies like Baxter, Bayer, and AstraZeneca to establish research centers in China. Overseas venture capitalists are actively seeking Chinese medical start-ups to invest in; over twelve thousand medical device manufacturers and one hundred forty-five thousand medical distributors are currently in operation in China.[7] With this attention, the government is watching medical companies, especially exporters of medical products and pharmaceuticals, like a hawk and will not let any person or company tarnish their growing reputation.

However, even with this said, the Chinese government still has many cracks in its armor. Just in 2007, the head of China's Food and Drug Administration was executed for taking bribes from Chinese pharmaceutical companies. Both private and state-owned drug makers have been accused of falsifying clinical test trial data and killing hundreds of patients with tainted drugs. But even with these horrific infractions and injustices, the medical industry is far cleaner than unregulated industries. The thousands of small mom-and-pop companies and factories producing electronics,

---

[7] Knowledgeatwharton.com.cn, "China's Healthcare Industry Is Hot, and Investors Are Paying Attention," last modified November 21, 2007.

toys, metal and plastic components, and household appliances are much more prone to committing fraud and producing shabby products.

The scrap metal trade is one of the shadiest businesses in China. The industry is a magnet for get-rich-quick scammers, tax-evading fugitives, and mafia-like characters. I should know, as I met many of them while trying to get money back for a scrap metal dealer in Los Angeles. The scrap metal industry is a cash business requiring hundreds of thousands of dollars, and business transactions are one-off deals, meaning relationships last for only a deal or two, no long-term contracts or kinship needed. This is a perfect scenario for rip-off artists. From 2006 to 2008, every Chinese Madoff-wannabe bought and sold scrap metal and made lots of money as scrap steel prices doubled from $300 per ton to over $600 per ton in six months.

When metal prices were going up, foreign dealers easily extended credit to the Chinese buyers, and for the most part, they got paid back. After all, with 50 and 100 percent margins, the Chinese gladly paid their bills. But when prices plummeted in the midst of the financial crisis, the Chinese fled, leaving the foreign dealers and scrap metal literally on the docks. Be very cautious with industries that share common characteristics with the scrap metal business: low-tech requirements, low barriers to entry, little or no government oversight, cash transactions, commodity pricing, and an overabundant number of suppliers. Industries that fit this description include all consumer-related products, electronic components, plastics, low-tech household appliances, medical disposables, and furniture.

Company Morale

Employee morale is another key factor in deciding a company's trustworthiness and long-term sustainability. The happier the rank and file, the better the owners and management are treating them. Low morale, high turnover rates, and union complaints from many workers are signs that managers are mistreating, cheating, and abusing employees. If they cheat their employees, you can bet your bottom dollar that customers and business partners are also victims.

As part of a quality inspection team, I visited one of Foxconn Electronics' subsidiary manufacturing facilities in southern China in 2007. Foxconn, one of the world's largest electronic components manufacturers and assemblers, employs over two hundred thousand workers in the Shenzhen area. I walked by one of the many employee dormitories and saw a local labor union telephone number listed on a bulletin board. After I left the premises, I called the number. A union representative took my call. She was somewhat skeptical when I told her who I was and my purpose for calling, which was to inquire about general work conditions and morale at Foxconn for one my outsourcing clients. After some persuasion, she and some of her colleagues agreed to meet with me.

Once we broke the ice and they realized I was not a company spy, I could not stop them from talking. The upshot was this: management treated factory workers inhumanely. Line workers were forced to work overtime without extra pay; some were beaten when accused of stealing components; unwarranted firings were a daily event; and security guards treated employees like convicts in a maximum-security prison.

After these startling revelations, I advised my large consumer electronics client not to work with Foxconn. This came as a surprise to my client since Foxconn was a world-class supplier to such companies as Cisco, Apple, and Huawei. I did not want my well-known client's electronic products built by line workers who were allegedly being physically and mentally abused. Of course, I had not seen actual evidence of this happening, but why take the chance?

My discoveries and recommendations were later substantiated when Apple conducted an audit at Foxconn's Shenzhen facilities in 2011. They found widespread cases of bribery, underage workers, chemical-related health problems, and doctored payroll documents. In March of 2012, Apple's CEO, Tim Cook, visited two of Foxconn's facilities in China and publically announced that both Apple and Foxconn will work together to improve working conditions.

Chapter 2 Summary

1. Foreigners tend to use Western standards—education, family background, and financial status—to judge whether a Chinese counterpart is trustworthy and a viable potential partner. Making an accurate judgment is virtually impossible given the vast cultural and language rifts between Chinese and Westerners.

2. Don't ever use your gut instincts to select a partner. Your gut doesn't work in China. Similarly, don't work with a partner just because you trust them. Westerners may be able to make instinctive decisions when dealing with their fellow countryperson, but they lack the experience needed to make similar judgments toward the Chinese.

3. Trusting your Chinese counterpart can lead to disastrous results. The Chinese, especially the Mao Generation ones, will eat you alive. I should know. I spend most of my consulting time unwinding these "trusting" relationships, which usually leave foreign companies in the dust.

4. Invariably, after telling my clients not to trust their Chinese counterparts, they still want to trust. So if you must rely on trust, examine chart 2.1, which describes methods to help you better judge Chinese individuals. Broadly speaking, you will have more in common with Chinese businesspeople with these characteristics: fluency in English, a college education, under the age of thirty-five, overseas work experience, and born and raised in one of the larger Chinese cities.

5. Chart 2.2 shows ways you can better judge the trustworthiness of Chinese companies. More trusting companies will have these characteristics: is involved in a government-controlled industry, has low employee turnover, has overseas customers, employs foreigners, and is located in a major city.

Chapter 3
The Translator: Your Only Link

For any China business trip, the Chinese-speaking member of your entourage will have the most important role, even more important than the vice president who tags along. The translator consultant serves as your only true communication link between two totally contrasting cultures. Your business savvy will only be as good as the translator's communication skills.

Unfortunately, foreign businesspeople give little or no consideration to this matter, thinking that either their hosts will have English-speaking personnel readily available or that translators can be easily hired on the fly. Neither option is advisable, and either could lead to failed business trips. Rather than using external resources, SMBs should be equipped in-house with proper talent, specifically people who can speak Chinese and who know the Chinese culture and mind-set. Further, this person should be well versed and experienced in your specific business and industry and thoroughly briefed on the trip objectives.

Three Important Roles

Most businesspeople view a translator's role as simply paraphrasing English into Chinese and vice versa. If they were only mimicking words, we could use one of the many translation software tools available in the marketplace. In reality, a translator's job entails many responsibilities, the easiest of which is the actual translation. Their responsibilities will encompass executive duties that require business experience, intuitive thinking, technical knowledge, and cultural sensitivities to both parties. A translator's tasks falls into three vital areas.

Role 1: Wearing Many Hats

The first task is serving as a full-blown representative for your company, since all eyes and ears will be centered on the translator. Wearing many hats—sales, quality, purchasing, and finance— the translator must be familiar with your company's business, industry, trip objectives, and specific reasons for each appointment in China. This is one of the reasons why you can't just pick up a translator from the *Shanghai Daily* classified ads section, which unfortunately many companies do.

Along the same lines, translators can provide advice and opinions on the meeting's progress and what additional issues should be brought up or, in some cases, not brought up. A personal experience illustrates this point. I was advising and providing translation services for an American environmental testing company on the possibility of buying a Chinese testing company in Shenzhen. We visited the company with the pretense of possibly outsourcing some of their testing services. As the day's meeting progressed, I found the Chinese owner to be rather arrogant, touting their skill sets and vast market share throughout China. Further, they talked about buying an American company to break into the North American market. Their attitude was not conducive for us to bring up a possible buyout, and I told my clients so. Bringing the subject up would have insulted them by giving them the impression that we were bigger and better than them. My American clients never picked up on these signals but respected my intuition. Though disappointed, they understood, and we left the matter for another time.

Role 2: Directing the Meeting

The second important role for the translator is the ability to steer the meeting and conversations to your side. Discussions in two languages can easily go off-course, leaving unfinished business and no clear-cut conclusions. I remember an incident with one of my German customers, who was visiting a laminated steel factory in Suzhou. Their main focus was to discuss manufacturing processes while the Chinese factory owner wanted to talk about pricing and purchase orders. Everybody was talking, no one was listening, and I was getting a headache. "Let's take a ten-minute break!" I took the owner aside and told him to relax, be patient, and we'd eventually get to pricing and orders just as soon we solved the manufacturing issues. He adhered, and things went more smoothly. A translator on your team will maintain the focus and gently remind the Chinese to stay on course. This will ensure that, at the end of the day, all answers and objectives are met.

Role 3: Reading between the Lines

Skilled translators can also pick up information in meetings that foreigners cannot readily hear or see. They may overhear side discussions by midlevel managers or catch certain tones, key words, or nuances in a factory manager's voice. In chapter 2, I listed criteria on ways to judge a Chinese businessperson's trustworthiness. Chinese often judge one another by their accents, which can reveal clues on family history or social class, though these are sometimes misleading. Someone from Xinjiang may be regarded as poor since the area mostly supports farming with little or no industrialization, whereas a Shanghai accent may be thought to show more prominence, education, and sophistication. Foreigners have no chance of catching these little nuances.

On an outsourcing trip, the factory owner took my American clients out for a typical night on the town: a huge Chinese banquet and KTV (karaoke television); these large, flashy entertainment centers for businesspeople (mostly businessmen) feature singing, private rooms, hostesses, and lots of drinking. Two things bothered me about the owner. He kept getting phone calls from someone demanding money. The owner persistently told the caller he would receive it by tomorrow. I couldn't hear exactly, but it sounded like he owed $100,000—an awful lot of money in China. The owner loved soccer and professed to lay down a wager every now and then, so maybe he had some gambling debts. Second, as we entered our private room, the *mama-san* greeted the owner and casually mentioned it was his eighth straight visit in as many nights. Later, I passed my observations on to my colleagues, who subsequently ceased business with the carousing owner. Large gambling debts, drinking, and womanizing are not a good match for the medical equipment manufacturing business. Again, this shows the importance of an experienced, savvy translator watching your back.

Bad Translators

Chinese companies will tell you before your visit that they have international sales staffs who are proficient enough in English. Typically, their writing skills are excellent, but their speaking ability is not adequate enough to carry out any complicated business discussions. They are familiar with English words associated with sales-related matters but have little expertise in other business subjects. Additionally, I would never want another company's employee speaking on my behalf. I won't know how the translator will represent me, and the translations are likely to be biased toward the Chinese company.

Another option is for SMBs to hire Chinese companies that provide translation services. They can be found in the many English newspapers in China (*Shanghai Daily, People's Daily*). These agencies provide many translation services related to business, sightseeing, and emergency medical and travel matters. I must give you fair warning, however; they provide very poor business translation services and will basically ruin any China business trip. It's difficult for me to understand how any foreign company wanting to make a serious effort in China, and willing to spend thousands of dollars to make a trip, will just casually cold call an unknown source for translation services. Going that route, you won't know the background, experience, or competence level of an interpreter who will serve as your company representative. Your translator is essentially your new best friend during the China trip, and I would never find a friend from the classified ads—at least I hope not.

In most cases, this is what the local Chinese translation companies will provide: a young person, typically a woman, who studied English at the university level and has several years of experience working as a tour guide or at an export/import company dealing with foreign customers. The person's English will be almost perfect, since she has spent much time conversing with tourists, but she will lack the business experience, knowledge, and specific industry expertise to do a proper job. And she will end up doing more harm than good.

One of my clients, a Korean water purifier manufacturer, used one of these services in Shanghai to meet potential distributors. As with most industries, the water purification business has its own terminology and jargon. Most of these specialized terms—*ionization, carbon blocking, reverse osmosis*—are chemistry related. The translator, a woman who had majored in English literature, did not even have the capacity to understand the equivalent Chinese technical terms, let alone the English words. Both the Koreans and Chinese had to explain the English and Chinese words before she was able to translate, taking sometimes up to an hour just to get a few sentences across. Needless to say, the business trip was frustrating for the Koreans. They may have saved some money in translation services, but they ultimately lost out in garnering any China business.

Another tendency of bad translators is to take over conversations, leaving you on the sidelines watching like a spectator. I have been in this situation when using translators in South Korea. I felt left out, ignored, and frustrated. For all I knew, they could be conspiring to cheat me. My translator would talk for half an hour in Korean, and then pause to give me a thirty-second synopsis; then he would go back to speaking in Korean for another hour. An experienced translator will keep all the participants engaged. He or she is in charge of the discussions: signaling a speaker when to speak and pause, asking listeners if they understood the translation, allocating time so all can have a say, and most of all, making sure the meeting objectives are being met. No question, this is a tough job, tougher than most people imagine and certainly not work you just find someone off the street to do.

Selecting a Translator

Now that we understand the role of the translator, it should be obvious that the best person for the job is an internal employee who has China experience and skills. A qualified candidate should possess the following: fluency in English and Mandarin, familiarity with your business and industry, and living and working experience both in China and your home country.

Ignoring these required qualifications can lead to a poor hire. Just because someone looks Chinese or speaks Chinese does not mean the candidate fulfills the necessary factors for success. Unfortunately, I have worked with many SMBs that made the mistake of thinking this way. Spectrogram, a medical stent and laser contract manufacturer based just outside of Minneapolis, used one of their executive vice presidents to take the lead on their China trips. No doubt, John was very knowledgeable in Spectrogram's businesses; he also had a PhD in physics, so he was equally proficient on the technical side. He could easily represent the company on all fronts.

John's resume for China, however, was misleading. On the surface, he was a good candidate to handle business there; after all, he had been born in Asia, and he spoke Chinese. But let's dig a little deeper. John had immigrated to the United States over twenty-five years before from Hong Kong. Since then he had never visited China or done any business there. His mother tongue, Cantonese, though linguistically considered a dialect of Mandarin Chinese, is completely different and incomprehensible to Mandarin speakers. John also lacked any real-life, hands-on Chinese business experience to help him effectively mediate and translate conversations. He was no better than a foreign businessperson having zero China experience and Chinese-language skills.

SMBs also make the mistake of hiring overseas Chinese—Singaporeans, Malaysians, or Indonesians—to act as their China mediator. The assumption that they are the same as mainland Chinese is not correct. Take Singaporean Chinese as an example: They live in Asia, travel to China frequently for pleasure, speak many dialects of Mandarin, and share similar cultures as mainlanders. To unsuspecting foreigners, Singaporeans and mainland Chinese are exactly the same. But mainlanders view Singaporeans as hybrid Chinese. They don't speak Mandarin very well and do so with heavy, sometimes incomprehensible, accents; eat pseudo Chinese food blended with Indian, Malay, and Indonesian ingredients; and live in a mostly Westernized community, speaking English and watching English television shows. One could even argue that Singaporeans are more British than Chinese, Singapore having once been a British colony. Their educational and legal systems are British-based, they drive on the right-hand side of the road, and the city still retains much of the old British colonial architecture.

Zhang Jianbo is a local Chinese businessman, based in Shanghai and working at Sungard China, a leading international services company. He routinely deals with overseas Chinese. "I don't understand why foreign companies always send Singaporeans to China. They speak Chinese funny, don't understand how we do business, and always think they are better than us, telling us how to do things. We are two totally different countries. I'd rather work with a complete Westerner; at least they fully admit their ignorance about China."

SMBs may not have the budget necessary to hire an in-house China expert, so another solution would be to hire a consultant like me. There are, however, drawbacks in using third parties. For one, they may not have the necessary expertise in your specific industry. My organization, for example, can handle only certain industries: medical, automotive, information technology, and manufacturing. Another shortcoming is the lack of familiarity with the consultant and vice versa. Do you really want to gamble your China plans on a stranger? Make an effort to train your consultant as you would a new employee in areas like understanding the company culture, developing relationships with key personnel, and knowing your products inside and out.

Though I am totally against it, SMBs may still want to go the inexpensive route and hire local translators. If this must be done, at least adhere to the following advice: Make a visit to the translation company's office, describe your company's industry and purpose for visiting China, and interview the translators. After a translator has been chosen, spend a couple of hours with the candidate detailing the objectives of the upcoming meetings and trying to make him or her feel at ease with you. Most of all, instruct the translator that you value any opinions, observations, or insight that you, as a foreigner, may not notice.

Working with Your Translator

Meetings with translators are quite different from typical English-only meetings. They are slower, taking three to four times longer than single-language meetings. Dialogues are choppy because each speaker has to stop in the middle of the conversation to wait for the translator. This often disrupts your train of thought. Even worse, the subject you wanted to discuss can pass, leaving you wondering if you should even speak up.

I always prepare my clients on how to handle translated meetings. Most important: keep conversations short, simple, and to the point.

When asked a question by your Chinese counterparts, respond as simply as you can—preferably with a yes or no answer—before diving into the details. This will perk the non-English-speaking attendees' attentions. They now know the general direction of the conversation as they wait patiently for the long answer. Americans are not accustomed to these short comments or answers. Chinese businesspeople (and Europeans as well) complain that Americans talk too much. One of my Chinese-born colleagues told me, "You guys [Americans] talk everything to death. Sometimes I just want a simple yes or no, but instead I get a thirty-minute speech. Or I want to know about subject matter A, and I get a lecture about subject A, B, and C. I just want to scream and yell, 'Stop!'"

I recall one incident when a Chinese factory owner asked his American counterpart what the revenue-sharing percentage breakdowns would be between them. Instead of a simple answer, the American went on about his philosophical views on business and how successful he planned to be in China. I sensed he was just too embarrassed to quote a number, not wanting the Chinese to think he was greedy. Finally, he reluctantly gave a number which brought forth further discussions and an eventual deal. In such a situation, either give a straight answer or ask for some more time to consider an appropriate response. This posturing back and forth wastes time, confuses the Chinese, and makes for a difficult translation.

Another key tip is to not interrupt the translator. Allow the translator to finish the speaker's thoughts and then pause for a few seconds to see if the speaker wishes to continue. Too often the translator gets cut off. Americans like to interject with questions or offer their unsolicited and often opposing opinions instantaneously, without concern for the other party.

Ask more questions of your Chinese partners than you normally would in English-only meetings. "Are you sure you understand?" "Should I repeat anything?" Your counterparts may be too shy or embarrassed to ask for clarification, so your questions may initiate further discussions. Also ask the translator questions: "Are you sure this is what they meant?" "I didn't understand the last part—could you repeat that?" A good translator will clarify the matter immediately or at least pose the issue to the speaker again.

Lastly, take more restroom breaks and huddle up with your team and translator. Make sure everybody agrees with the previously discussed points and formulate new agendas for the next session. This would be a good time for your translator to add insight and between-the-lines information. Nuances like facial expressions, the use of certain words, or attitudes can be valuable information that only a Chinese-speaking person can catch. I recall one incident in which we were negotiating prices for some industrial equipment. As the Chinese manager was quoting me prices, I could see another manager across the table jotting down what I believed to be their minimum prices and quantity levels in Chinese. I quickly called a bathroom break and informed my European customers. We now had their rock-bottom pricing from which to negotiate. I earned my consulting fees on that trip!

Chapter 3 Summary

1. The translator is the most important person on your China business trip. A bad translator will ruin any trip.

2. Never hire translators from a Chinese newspaper's classified advertisements. They usually have no business skills, and their English is, at best, conversational. Never use your Chinese counterpart's English-speaking employees, either; their English is typically not proficient enough for business discussions—and why would you ever want representatives from another company speaking on your behalf?

3. An excellent translator will have these characteristics: lived and worked in China; astute knowledge of your business; some working experience in basic business functions, such as accounting, marketing, or operations; the ability to direct a meeting toward your goals; a keen sense of the macro issues and topics you want to accomplish; a knack for reading between the lines; and an awareness of the many background conversations going on in a meeting.

4. It's always best to have your own in-house translator. Better yet, hire a Chinese-speaking person for one of your key management positions.

5. Help your translator out in meetings: Get to the point. Don't ramble on and on. Allow the translator to finish one translation before moving on to your next point. Ask lots of

questions, making sure both the translator and the Chinese partner understand your comments.

6. Take a lot of meeting breaks so you can huddle with your translator. The translator can then feed you any inside information accidentally overheard, opinions on how things are moving along, and suggestions for the next session.

Chapter 4
Throw Away the Contract

It's not fair to say that contracts with Chinese companies are useless, but foreign SMBs will have to treat contracts differently than how they normally view them in the West. They are not foolproof protection for your business. This chapter will discuss the current legal situation in China, how Chinese businesspeople view contracts, and why their perspectives are so different from those of Westerners. Later, in chapter 5, I'll go into the ways foreign SMBs can protect themselves with Chinese contracts as well as other nontraditional methods.

Disadvantage to SMBs

For large corporations, contracts are mostly adhered to in China, but not because the judicial system works. MNOs know it's a crapshoot as to whether any disputes will be resolved fairly in the courts. Rather, it's who you know, how much you invest, and how big you are that enforces contracts in China. China's central government and judicial systems are basically one and the same, meaning the state government heavily influences courts' decisions, usually in the government's favor. Therefore, the combination of political, monetary, and public pressure on Beijing is often a better route than going to the courts.

MNOs are investing billions into China and hiring hundreds of thousands of its people; they are a major factor in China's economic growth, and Beijing is well aware of that fact. As long as it fits their interests, the central government will do their best to appease them. When major disputes arise, MNOs will attack on both fronts by going to the courts as well as making calls to one of the many ministry heads or even to President Xi Jinping himself. The IBMs and General Electrics of the world have this kind of clout in China. Finally, if all else fails, the MNO may suggest to the state government that their $10 billion infrastructure investment may go to India instead. That should do the trick in resolving any major contractual issues.

The story, however, is very different for foreign SMBs. With no political or monetary power, SMBs have a difficult time enforcing Chinese contracts. As Americans, we have become accustomed to hiding behind the mumbo jumbo that the American legal system has graciously offered us. Legal principles like indemnification, punitive damages, force majeure, or injunctive relief are either nonexistent in Chinese law or exist but are rarely upheld or are difficult to enforce. The Chinese court system, judges, and local lawyers simply lack the experience and interpretative skills to translate what is on paper to real, day-to-day business situations. Most of the business-related laws serve as paper protection, resulting in a false pretense for foreigners that all is safe and secure. Remember, Dorothy, we are not in Kansas anymore.

Vague and Changing Laws

Many Chinese lawyers have told me that Chinese laws are written too vaguely, which makes them difficult to abide by and enforce. These loosely written laws allow for a wide range of interpretations. And when seeking clarification on a specific law, lawyers often don't know which government agency to go to, as several ministries may claim jurisdiction. What's more difficult is that these laws are constantly changing depending upon the mood swings and political agendas of the local and state governments.

"China's laws are continually changing and vague because our legal history is very short, only really starting in 1978 with China's Open Door Policy," claims Kevin Xu, partner at Martin Hu & Partners and graduate of Fudan University Law School, sometimes referred to as the Harvard of China. "We started off with just a legal framework in the eighties and early nineties [and] are now just working on the articles and subsets. We also do not have the experience and expertise to write laws, so this adds to the continuous changes. In fact, 70–80 percent of the laws I studied in law school are obsolete."

New Green Energy Laws

Laws are changed or added often without warning. Take the central government's recent interest in green technology and energy savings. Until recently, China had no concern for global warming, as it only wanted to expand its own economic prowess. In doing so, the state government gave large tax rebates to small- and medium-sized companies in China's largest industrial sectors: steel, mining, fertilizer, and oil. These tax rebates were basically subsidies to these weaker Chinese exporting companies, which allowed them to compete in the global markets. The companies benefiting from the tax rebate were all heavy carbon monoxide polluters, but China didn't care at that time.

Then suddenly in 2007, with little warning, China decreed it would no longer subsidize these high-pollutant manufacturers. No reason was given for this sudden reversal, but most China watchers believe it was a move to reduce both China's carbon footprint and to cool its double-digit GDP growth rates. The aftereffects were dramatic: thousands of heavy industry companies were either sold off or simply went belly-up. Companies were given no warning and no time to prepare for this setback.

This sudden policy reversal affected only domestic manufacturers, but other, future decisions could drastically alter the way foreign companies work in China. Just last year, China Mobile, the world's largest mobile carrier with over 600 million subscribers, asked Apple Computer to disengage iPods' Wi-Fi functionality before selling the devices in China. China Mobile and its owner, the government, are contemplating introducing indigenously innovated competing technologies for their domestic market. With this potential policy change, China could ban all Wi-Fi devices and hotspots, resulting in major chaos for foreigners, business travelers, and high-tech companies developing Wi-Fi products and services. Imagine thousands of Wi-Fi-related companies being shut out of the world's largest wireless market, possibly sending both sales and company stock prices plummeting.

Labor Laws
Beijing's policy and laws toward migrant workers are also continually changing. China today has basically a "see no evil" policy toward illegally using factory workers. Thousands of

factories cheat millions of workers by paying them below the legal minimum, offering them no overtime or mandatory welfare benefits, and firing them without cause. Provincial governments know this but choose to look the other way in favor of more taxes and a higher GDP. And thousands of foreign companies benefit from this agenda in the form of lower costs and higher profits for their shoes, sunglasses, and toys.

What if one day Beijing took a more compassionate stance toward its migrant labor force, changing its laws to ensure tighter control and stiffer punishments for companies who hire workers unlawfully? The world as we know it would be a different place. Prices for name-brand Chinese exports—from Nike shoes and Gap jeans to Whirlpool washers and HP printers—would increase dramatically, and foreign companies based in China for its cheap labor force would be forced to rethink their strategy, with many probably going belly-up. This could actually one day play out in real life. Beijing is currently in the process of lessening its dependence on manufacturing and exports, promoting more research and development and shifting to a consumer-based economy. To speed up this process, policy makers may seek to close low-tech factories while increasing wages and tightening labor laws, resulting in an immediate and negative impact on foreign companies operating in China.

Expatriating Funds

Expatriating money out of China is tightly controlled and monitored by the State Administration of Foreign Exchange (SAFE). They often, without notice, make sudden changes in the amount of funds that can be wired to and from China as a way to control both currency exchange rates and short-term banking reserves.

These sudden knee-jerk actions and reactions can create havoc for foreign SMBs needing cash. Typically at the end of a financial year or quarter, large MNOs may bring back their operating profits to the headquarters, requiring millions of renminbi (RMB)—the Chinese currency—to be exchanged for euros or dollars. It seems that SAFE freely allows large Chinese domestic companies and MNOs to repatriate funds but will limit both Chinese and foreign SMBs. MNOs will complain to Beijing if they can't bring back cash, so instead, they control and pressure SMBs, whose complaints will fall on deaf ears. This is just another example of MNOs and SMBs operating according to different rules in China, and thus having to come up with different game plans.

Take one incident, for example, in which a small US software company expected to receive a $30,000 wire transfer from their Chinese distributor for a software sale. The distributor, a small ten-employee company in Shenzhen, was temporarily banned from doing the transfer by their local bank. The bank gave no reasons and told them to come back in a few weeks. This created a big problem for the American company. The transfer was required before the end of the year to fulfill the distributor's annual quota to maintain exclusivity. The American company was upset and threatened to end the relationship, but the Shenzhen company argued that the situation was beyond their control. In reality, no one was at fault; the Chinese company wanted to pay, but couldn't. The American company, not understanding the oddities of China, wrongly assumed their Chinese counterpart was trying to cop out of the deal.

Too Many Cooks in the Kitchen
Another contributing factor to the ambiguity of China's legal system lies in the many government ministries that claim

responsibility for the same laws. The 2008 milk scandal—involving dairy products that were tainted with melamine, a chemical used to manufacture plastics and fertilizer, to artificially boost the protein—is a prime example. Over thirteen thousand babies throughout China were hospitalized, and at least four confirmed deaths were reported. Before the scandal, four government agencies claimed responsibility for China's food quality: the Ministry of Health, the Ministry of Commerce, the Ministry of Industry, and the General Administration of Quality Supervision, Inspection, and Quarantine (GAQSIQ). When asked who was responsible for this matter, each ministry passed the buck to the other. Beijing has since clearly defined the roles: the Ministry of Health controls all food-related manufacturing, the Ministry of Commerce monitors food sales, and GAQSIQ handles all food-quality issues. At least some good has come out of this horrific incident.

Xu has had many difficulties dealing with the multitude of ministries and their bureaucracies. "We are heading toward better clarity, but there still remain many conflicts. When you do something wrong, many ministries or departments will punish or fine you. But when you need assistance, nobody takes responsibility, telling you to go to another agency."

In Theory, but Not Practice

Chinese business law, though still needing modernization and updating, is better than most people think. There are laws for any business-related subject: copyright, company registration, patents, work safety, and labor. In theory the current laws should be enough to govern and decide most business conflicts, but unfortunately what is on paper is not often practiced. Legislating is one thing; implementing and enforcing the laws are another.

The thousands of municipalities that hold responsibility for enforcing decrees from Beijing simply lack the time, experience, know-how, and interest to properly enforce white-collar crimes at this early stage of China's economic development. They have more pressing matters—pollution, political corruption, social unrest, and energy and raw material shortages—to worry about than a foreign company's financial mishaps.

China's copyright and trademark laws are clear: one cannot copy commercial CDs or reproduce brand-name clothing. However, as we all know, nothing could be further from the reality. I typically stay at the Hilton Hotel when in Shanghai and can walk no more than one hundred yards from the hotel and see at least two or three people hawking fake movie DVDs. In October of 2009 I saw fake DVDs for the movie *Avatar*—a good two months before the movie debuted in the States.

In 2007, *Fortune* magazine wrote that 90 percent of China's 120 million personal computers had pirated software installed, mostly with Microsoft's operating system. I know vast improvements have been made since then, but I can still go into government offices and SOEs and see pirated software running on their computers. How do I know? I simply ask, and employees tell me without hesitation or guilt. On my same visit to Shanghai, Microsoft's new operating system, Microsoft 7, was available to purchase for about one hundred RMB (about fifteen dollars) from local hawkers standing outside the Shanghai Hilton.

For public relations purposes only, local authorities raid CD factories from time to time, accompanied by television crews and local politicians. These made-for-television roundups are usually done before international events like the Olympics and the World's Fair or visits from US dignitaries. Unfortunately, they have virtually no impact on this multibillion-dollar black market.

Local Governments Pick and Choose the Laws They Enforce

The reason a large discrepancy exists between laws that just sit on the books and ones that actually are enforced lies in the separation of powers between the central and the provincial or local governments. To put things simply, the central government proposes and makes laws for all of China. It is then up to the provincial governments to enforce the laws. Much of the time, the local governments do not have adequate resources to enforce all the laws on the books. Other times, they'll pick and choose the laws that are favorable to their city's best interest or their own pockets. This is nothing different from in the United States where the federal, state, and local governments often don't see eye to eye. China just takes things to the extreme.

Local municipalities, such as Shanghai or Shenzhen, simply do not have the incentive to go after the hundreds of makeshift factories producing pirated software and consumer goods. In fact, it's just the opposite. Many of these factories actually pay taxes, produce other legitimate products, and employ thousands of workers who would otherwise be on the streets committing crimes. Another reason why authorities look the other way is that many Chinese don't see copyright infringement as a real, legitimate crime. After all, who's the victim? Microsoft? Disney Studios? Chinese don't see them as victims; rather, they might be viewed as culprits, using and abusing Chinese sweatshops and making billions off Chinese consumers while giving nothing back. I don't share this view, but I can see how some Chinese might.

But one day, when Chinese companies start seeing their creative works stolen in Western countries, when they see actual money stolen from their pockets, Beijing will begin to take copyright infringement seriously. And I suspect that day will come in the next ten to fifteen years as China conforms itself from a low-cost producing country to a more innovative, technology-driven one. China is on the precipice of evolving from "research and copy" to "research and develop."

Chinese labor laws are another apt example of how municipalities choose and pick the laws they want to enforce. In January of 2008, the National People's Congress enacted the Labor Contract Law, which stipulated tighter regulations on firing workers, allowed for severance packages, and mandated written contracts for workers at all pay-scale levels. This was a very positive sign from Beijing, and many labor watchdog organizations from around the world applauded the move.

At first, the new law created improvements in the factory workplace: wages and benefits went up, work conditions improved, and unwarranted layoffs were reduced. The state media promoted the new legislation, which created a jump in labor complaints. The city of Dongguan alone received more than sixty thousand complaints in 2008, more than double the amount in the previous two years.[8] The city's resources were overloaded, creating delays in the arbitration process.

These delays created additional problems. First, factory workers were not paid while their complaints were stuck in limbo, but

---

[8] Sky Canaves, "Factory Closures Strain China's Labor Law," *Wall Street Journal*, January 17, 2009.

most could not afford living without a paycheck. Workers then simply abandoned their grievances, opting to find other work or return home to the countryside. Second, the extra time allowed factory owners to simply close down their existing operations thereby voiding out the complaints. Of course, they set up new factories just as quickly as they closed others down.

Many municipalities are turning a blind eye toward enforcing the new labor laws, claiming the laws are increasing labor costs and causing forced factory shutdowns, thereby reducing their tax revenues and GDP. On top of that, due to the 2008 financial crisis, thousands of factories throughout China went belly-up. There was unrest in the streets as unemployed migrant workers protested and loitered in the cities' train stations. Today many unscrupulous entrepreneurs are undermining the law by opening "shadow factories." These factories are unregistered and are usually located in old, dilapidated buildings hidden from public view and city officials. The owner then hires undocumented workers, paying them well below the minimum wages—and, of course, without offering benefits or overtime pay. They do not pay taxes and often bribe city officials to look the other way.

Enacting Old Laws

However, just because some laws are not enforced now doesn't mean things will continue that way. It all depends on the current political, economic, and socioeconomic situation, which dictates whether some laws will go into hibernation, while others suddenly, without notice, jump back on the government's priority list. Here is an example of how greed brought back an old law: China's film industry, backed by the central government, debuted a film titled *Confucius* during Chinese New Year in February 2010. To combat China's corruption problems, President Hu Jintao made it a priority to bring back Confucian principles teaching social harmony and respect for elders. *Confucius*, a high-budget film starring Hong Kong action hero Chow Yun-Fat, was supposed to be a big hit during the Chinese holiday season.

Millions went to the theater, but it was to see *Avatar*, the Oscar-nominated 3-D thriller that broke all box office records in 2009. Theaters quickly added more start times for *Avatar* but such a move meant reducing airtime for *Confucius*. China's state council, trying to save face and also make a buck, decreed that all theater operators needed to reserve two-thirds of all screen time for Chinese-made films. This law was actually on the books for many years, but it was never enforced until Beijing deemed it necessary for its own gain and advantage.

So to foreign SMBs, let this be an example to follow all laws. You never know when an old law will come back to bite you. Keep abreast of your specific industry regulations, because your current legal activities may turn out to be unlawful someday. Chinese laws and regulations change as fast as the whims of Beijing, and the enforcement of these laws literally varies quarter to quarter as the local provincial governments' coffers go up or down.

Cultural Differences

Many Chinese SMB owners actually do not use contracts when doing business with other Chinese, preferring to rely on personal relationships, face-saving tactics, and business savvy to mediate terms. The Chinese do understand contracts are a necessity when dealing with foreigners, but many actually do not consider them legal and binding obligations as we do in the West. They are viewed more as demonstrations of good faith symbolizing both the personal and business bonds between two parties. Along with dinners, toasting, and gift giving, the contract signing signifies an act of friendship, the beginning of a long-lasting relationship. Chinese managers will often casually sign without ever having read the details, assuming issues and conflicts can later be negotiated and discussed. Any hard negotiations before the signing could just create tension and bad feeling, so they prefer to just sign and get off to a good start. They think, *We'll work out the details later.*

I recall one incident in which a Chinese solar module manufacturer signed an agreement with an American solar systems integrator. The integrator required specialized modules having smaller footprints with higher power capacities. After six months of delays, the manufacturer admitted to not having the engineering skills to produce the specialized modules. The Americans were dumbfounded. Why would the manufacturer sign a contract when it could not meet product and test specifications? Worst yet, the contract included penalty fees for shipping delays, but of course, the Chinese had never bothered to read the details.

"We signed the contract to show our friendship and loyalty to our customer," said the solar manufacturer's president. "We had good intentions and planned to have the product before the deadlines. We never intentionally misled them. It's the opposite—we want to be friends first and business partners second."

Agree Today, but Not Tomorrow

There is another major difference in how the Chinese view contracts. When Chinese businesspeople sign the dotted line, they are agreeing to the terms; but this agreement is seen as only a snapshot in time. In other words, they agree to the conditions today but may not adhere to them next month or next year depending upon changing circumstances and events that adversely or positively affect the overall business. Foreigners have difficulty understanding this concept, but it actually makes good sense. How can we predict raw material prices or gauge consumer spending habits twelve months from today?

Rather than both parties sticking to some hard, written rules, we should negotiate and make compromises as economic conditions, supply and demand, and spending habits change over the course of time. This is regularly done among Chinese businesspeople. The keys for this to work are constant communication, a clear understanding of one another's sensitive issues, mutual respect, and the recognition that a win-win situation is, as the term implies, good for everybody.

For example, a Chinese buyer of computer memory boards makes it a point to know all too well the sensitive issues for his manufacturing partner, such as memory chip prices, rare earth metal supplies, and air-freight charges. Similarly, the manufacturer remains vigilant to his buyer's needs: timely delivery schedules, quality, and low prices. The two have developed a symbiotic relationship; it is not a winner-take-all situation as we often see in Western business relations. They know each other like the backs of their own hands. This is no accident. They meet and talk on a frequent basis, at least once a week. They dine together, get drunk together, and womanize together. And this is why dinners, karaoke, and drinking—activities that foreigners don't pay too much attention to—sometimes serve as important business tools.

In another example, I assisted a Minnesota-based medical company on an outsourcing project with a Wenzhou syringe manufacturer. The in-house lawyer for the American company presented the Chinese owner, Mr. Hongjie Zhang, with a sixty-page contract with all the Western legalese one would expect. Usually, the other side would take weeks to review and red ink such a long and verbose contract. Not Mr. Zhang, however. We received the contract by fax the next day with some minor technical specification changes but no major business-related amendments. Mr. Zhang also signed and faxed the signature page. Everything was complete.

Our lawyer was shocked. In all his dealings with outsourcing partners, he had never seen a factory agree to late delivery penalties or surprise quality audits. They usually counter with lower penalty charges and at least a week's warning for inspections. The lawyer asked me to check with Mr. Zhang to confirm his acceptance on these various issues. Zhang said, "For the contract, I was only interested in the price, quantities, shipping dates, technical drawings, materials used, and shipping methods. I did not review anything else because I don't consider them important; I'm sure we can discuss those other points when we come to it. We'll figure out a way to resolve any problems as they come, but why worry about a situation if it may never come up?"

Let's Renegotiate!

For yet another situation, let's go back to my American software vendor who was negotiating a contract with a Shenzhen distributor. The distributor had been courting the software developer for many months, claiming that China could be the biggest market in the world for them if they only gave the distributor a chance.

They demanded exclusivity, and in return, promised some hefty quarterly sales quotas. My client thought this was fair. The distributor had all of China, a low price, and fat profit margins. In return, the software vendor would double its Asian revenue in less than eighteen months.

Unfortunately, the distributor did not meet the first-quarter numbers. I went to Shenzhen to meet with them. Johnman, the general manager, in a demeaning manner, explained to me, "We are having a tough time selling the software due to local competitors. It also takes time to sell a new brand in China. We'll need better pricing, a lower quota, and some marketing development funds. And we still must have exclusivity or we will have no means of protecting the market."

Johnman's attitude was very matter-of-fact. He showed no remorse, nor was he apologetic. It was as if he expected me to understand his situation, take what he said as the complete truth, and continue on with the relationship without him having to make any concessions. I queried him as to whether he felt obligated to meet the contractual terms. "Yes, it was our intention to at the time of signing. But you have to understand things have changed in three months, and the contract doesn't apply to these new conditions. You just don't understand what a difficult time we are having. Let's prepare a new contract!"

Any foreign businessperson would have fired Johnman on the spot. How dare he renege on the contract and then have the audacity to ask for better pricing? It is important to not get mad, but instead, to have backup plans for when—not if—your Chinese partner decides to change the contract terms (I discuss more of this in chapter 7). This incident, though frustrating and time-consuming for my software vendor, was actually not so bad given that it only involved software, an invisible product that had no shipping or storage costs. I've had similar contract disputes involving millions of dollars' worth of hard assets (such as automobile parts, medical equipment, or industrial machinery) sitting in the warehouses of Chinese companies. And in some cases, the products had yet to be paid for since the Chinese partners were given payment terms. The Chinese had their Western partners in a stranglehold. Renegotiate the contract, or get no money or equipment back.

Legacy of Corruption

In the West, we sign contracts because we know a fair and unbiased arbitrator, the court system, exists to mediate between two parties in the case of a disagreement. A court's only interest is to serve justice regardless of the size, affiliations, and relationships of the plaintiff or defendant. Some of my consulting clients are large Fortune 500 companies. In every way they are bigger than me, and they employ better lawyers, befriend government officials and politicians, and possess unlimited financial resources. But our judicial system will treat me and the Goliaths equally, and that's why I feel comfortable signing a contract with them.

Not so in China. The Communist government, SOEs, and court system are all intertwined. They can basically be viewed as one large entity—just having different faces and names. They all report to the same boss somewhere up the food chain. As recently as ten or fifteen years ago, privately held companies, foreign and Chinese alike, were certain to lose almost any battle in China, as the court's main objective was to protect, serve, and oversee the government's best interest. Things have changed since then, as

Beijing has become more socially, ethically, and morally conscious as it tries to abolish government-related corruption, including politically motivated decisions by the courts.

The Internet has also played a large role; Chinese citizens can openly and anonymously voice their opinions through the many blogs and social websites. The Me Generation, in their twenties and thirties, have become especially vocal about human rights, equality, the right to know, and justice for all. Any inkling of wrongdoing by the government and the courts would almost immediately be broadcast throughout China's Internet cafés and blogospheres. Beijing, in its own way, does listen and react.

I was in Shanghai on July 28, 2011, when a Chinese high-speed train crashed near Wenzhou, killing thirty-nine passengers. What I saw on CNN was appalling. Earth-moving tractors were digging large crater-like holes next to the crash site while large cranes were lifting and dumping the wrecked passenger cars into the holes. It was as if the government was scurrying to hide all the evidence before the reporters and news agencies got to the scene. This was immediately picked up by Chinese bloggers. Chinese citizens were outraged—mad as hell at the Chinese government. Just as quickly as the evidence was buried, Premier Wen Jiabao made a public statement saying there would be an "independent" investigation as to the cause of the crash. Days later, three government officials were sacked, and a preliminary report was issued stating that the cause was likely due to a design flaw in the signaling system.

But even with these revolutionary changes, most Chinese still don't trust the government and anything associated with it—banks, the judicial system, police, and even SOEs. I still meet locals who hide their cash in large, antique ceramic vases usually used to store so-called thousand-year-old preserved eggs. Contracts, too, are just another tool for the government to use and abuse. Government corruption has been a part of China for over two thousand years, so it will take some time before attitudes change.

The Mao Generation

Much of this distrust toward the government and related institutions goes back to the Cultural Revolution. As I discuss in earlier chapters, the Communist government under Mao ruthlessly dictated and undermined its citizens. Most historians categorize Mao's reign into two distinct eras. The first, the Great Leap Forward in the 1950s, was designed to have peasants form collective households or communes to share farm equipment and produce agricultural products, of which the Communist government would take a portion for its own use and resale. Rich landowners were forced to give up their land to the government for "the good of the people." During this period, over five hundred thousand Chinese were executed or died in jails, and an estimated twenty to forty million others died of starvation due to failed government policies. The Great Leap Forward was a complete disaster, causing both political leaders and citizens to distrust their government to the point that Mao was forced to give up part of his control.

The second period, the Cultural Revolution (1966–1977), created further destruction and distrust of the government. Mao wanted to purge the Communist Party of capitalists and the "liberal bourgeois." This included educators, land and business owners, and anybody who had previously worked or lived in Western countries. Mao formed the Red Guards, the group responsible for sending "criminals" to the countryside for reeducation. They were typically young and uneducated people who marched into cities preaching the wisdom of Mao. They taught children to distrust their parents and confess any anti-Mao rhetoric coming from friends, family, or neighbors. Books were burned, Confucianism was ridiculed, and Western ideology was deemed corrupt.

Imagine children at that time being told by government officials to rat on their parents, grandparents, and teachers. What were they to think? Who were they to believe? Yet nothing good came from listening to the government, just poverty, hate, and destitution. The children of the Cultural Revolution, the Mao Generation, are now in their forties and fifties; they own businesses, travel abroad, hold government positions, manage factories, and work as engineers and salespeople. Being exposed to many years of mostly institutional corruption—bribery scandals, high officials stealing from pension funds, nepotism, cronyism, and unscrupulous bank loans—has led them to doubt the legitimacy of the government, including its courts and laws. Without trust in the legal system, Chinese businesspeople will never have faith in contracts or the people who enforce them, but instead will continue to rely on personal contacts and immediate family.

I often speak to my relatives who suffered dearly during Mao's reign. I see the pain in their faces as they describe the past horrors. Their youth was filled with despair and total waste. I feel compassion and empathize with them; they are my relatives, my bloodline. I care for them, but I don't think they reciprocate the same feelings. I don't believe they are capable of that. My father escaped to Taiwan, making the right decision, while they stayed behind, making the wrong decision. To make up for this, they live vicariously through me. They ask me how big my house is, what kind of car I own, how much money I have in the bank. They want what I have and feel no shame asking me for it. They don't treat me like family; there's no trust. I'm just a mirage of what they could have become but never will.

Chapter 4 Summary

1. China's legal system has made vast improvements over the past twenty years. Unfortunately, the laws are still vague, continually changing, and difficult to enforce. China still has a generation or two to go to before they will be able to catch up to the West.

2. In the meantime, SMBs should be weary of Chinese contracts, as they are not foolproof protection for your business. You must seek other means of protection.

3. Whether a Chinese contract is enforceable depends on who the Chinese counterpart is. If it's another SMB, there's little chance of even getting to court, as the owner will probably close up shop and simply disappear. You have a better chance with an SOE. But remember, the SOE and China's judicial system are basically one and the same; the courts will more than likely side with the SOE.

4. The fact that China's laws are difficult to enforce doesn't give you carte blanche to run amuck in China. On the contrary, stick to the letter of the law so there's no chance you can get in trouble. China, in a moment's notice, may decide to crack down on previously unenforced laws.

5. The Chinese view contracts as a goodwill gesture or a showing of cooperation, not as a firm commitment. They have no qualms about changing terms at a later date.

6. The Mao Generation Chinese have little appetite for contracts. To them, contracts are just another corrupt instrument of the government. Of course, they'll still sign your contract, but this generation has seen too much government corruption to believe in their country's judicial system.

Chapter 5
So, How Do We Protect Ourselves?

Still Need Something in Writing

If the concept of contracts varies so much between Chinese and Westerners, then why even bother to draw one up? For one, your management, investors, and lawyers will probably demand a contract. It's our culture to have a contract, and we will never get away from it. Second, your Chinese counterpart will want at least the major items (price, quantity, payment terms, and delivery schedule) documented in some form or another. It may come in different ways—in an e-mail, on a paper napkin, or by fax—and at different times, but for the Chinese, they all serve as confirmation that a business relationship exists.

And lastly, it's just good common sense to have the basics in writing. "You always want to start off on the right foot, so get a proper contract together with your partner," says Christopher Wright. "If problems arise, though you may not be able to go the courts, you can still at least draw on the contract as a reference point to negotiate with your Chinese counterparts. It's just decent business practice to have something in writing."

Chinese-Language Contracts

When in China, do as the Chinese do. To me that means making it as easy as possible for Chinese businesspeople to work and understand foreigners. We already do this without thinking, using translators or eating with chopsticks, but for some reason, we fail when it comes to contracts; they're always in English.

We need to take a lesson from the MNOs. They have the money, time, and resources to draft dual-language contracts, and often make the Chinese-language contract the official, working document that could potentially be used in court or arbitration. This seems very sensible, providing another layer of protection for foreigners.

To be fair to both sides, Kevin Xu, lawyer and partner at Martin Hu & Partners in Shanghai, recommends both contracts carry equal weight. But ultimately, Xu suggests to foreigners that they get to know the Chinese version better. "The bottom line is that the Chinese courts will refer to the Chinese-language contract as the official copy. After all, you are in China, and Chinese, both oral and written, is used in the courts."

Governing Law and Arbitration

Foreign lawyers representing foreign SMBs seemingly always require that a contract's governing law be that of the SMB's home state or country. This is a false sense of protection. There are only two locations where you can sue: your home country or China. Suing at home will make it virtually impossible to enforce any judgment, since foreign courts have no jurisdiction over a Chinese-based company. China does not have treaties with Western countries for recognizing a foreign court's decision.

And if you sue in China, a Chinese judge will read the Chinese contract and base his or her judgment on Chinese law, regardless of the governing law.

"The practicality of the matter," says Xu, "is that the judge, educated in China, only knows Chinese law and will make judgments using Chinese law. After all, that's all he knows. Of course, he will do his best to apply the country jurisdiction, but I think ultimately they will prefer to use Chinese law."

Rather than even bother to choose a country as the governing law, Xu recommends adding an arbitration clause to the contract. China is a member of the New York Convention, which means China's courts will recognize and enforce a decision made by one of the many approved international arbitration committees. Basically, the Chinese will treat the decision just as if a domestic Chinese court rendered the verdict. Chinese companies having international experience may insist on using their local committee, China International Economic and Trade Arbitration Commission, but Xu prefers either the Hong Kong International Arbitration Centre or the Singapore International Arbitration Centre. This will all but guarantee a fair judgment with no mainland Chinese influence in the decision-making process. Costs vary but in general are very reasonable and dependent upon the disputed amount. An arbitration case worth $500,000 will run about $40,000 in costs and fees.

Highlight Life-or-Death Issues

Somewhere in the contract, hopefully in the first few pages, should be a clear description of the essential elements of the relationship. This can take the form of short bullet-point comments. Take a distributorship contract for example; the details should include: price, quantity, quotas, payment terms, relationship duration, sales territory, descriptions of products, potential reasons to cease the relationship, and any other major points that are deemed vital to the relationship. Chances are this will be the only section a Chinese partner will read.

Just to be sure, go over each of these items in a face-to-face meeting and have your Chinese partner verbally acknowledge and accept the terms. I mean that you should literally ask them if they agree to each of the terms and listen for a reply, "Yes, I agree to the terms." This is important. I have been involved in discussions in which a Chinese partner confirmed the understanding of specific terms, but later after signing the contract, came back to say they did not agree to the terms. I guess they assumed we were just considering business options and they were agreeing to the different options. Anyway, I think you understand my point: make sure your partner knows the specific points exist and are vital for the relationship's future.

Lastly, at the end of the summary pages, list the conditions that allow a party to change any of the main points. I clearly put in writing and confirm again by verbally explaining to my Chinese partner that any contract changes cannot be made without the written consent of both parties. Some Chinese like to use a type of self-declared force majeure, citing changing market conditions or material costs as reasons to unilaterally alter terms.

In one case, a Chinese distributor sent us a purchase order with lower pricing, explaining that the competition had lowered pricing so they assumed we would match it. This could have been avoided if we had added the clause, "Neither party shall make price reductions unless both parties mutually agree to the change."

Contract Period

China is in constant flux, so you never want to tie yourself down for too long. Give yourself room to maneuver and react to the changing business environments. Because of this, I put a contract's duration, especially with a new and untested partner, to no more than twelve months. After gaining experience with a distributor or supplier, you can then extend the agreement to eighteen months, but certainly no more than two years. Time runs faster in China; twelve months may seem like two or three years in the West. Many things can change—poorly performing distributors, supplier quality issues, payment problems, changing business laws, material shortages, management changes, or currency and political instability. Anyone of these variables may give you reason to pull out of China, change partners or find new ones, or implement an altogether new action plan.

The more time you spend in China, the more you will learn, so having a short contract period will allow you to keep new options available as they arise, and they definitely will. You may meet the best distributor in one visit, but then another latest and greatest will come along the following year. Contrary to conventional wisdom, Chinese businesspeople, especially Chinese SMB owners, are also short-term thinkers who prefer fast, easy money over slow, continuous growth and long-lasting relationships. So in most cases, Chinese companies will also ask for short-term contracts to better gauge you, the market conditions, and the future. I would particularly worry if your Chinese counterpart asks for a longer-term relationship of more than two or three years. They must know something you don't, which means you will invariably be on the losing end.

Here's one example: In late 2006, I assisted several wealthy Chinese coal mine owners on a business trip to Australia. These savvy Chinese were offering to buy various types of coal at 10 percent above coal spot prices and wanted contracts for two to three years out. On top of that, they bought all the mining equipment, new or used, they could get their hands on. Everything they saw—underground conveyers, hauling equipment, bolters—they bought.

I didn't think much of it until I started writing this book. I checked the prices for Australian thermal coal, and prices went from about $71,000 per metric ton in July of 2007 to the peak of $200,000 in July of 2008. They made a killing and obviously had known something the Aussies and I hadn't. I called them to ask about it, but they said they had just made a bet on a hunch and gotten lucky. I doubt that very much. Wealthy Chinese are usually well connected with the government, and my guess is that they knew Beijing was increasing steel production for their many infrastructure and industrial projects (road construction, automobiles, and buildings). There was just no reason for them to sign long-term contracts at higher prices unless they had inside information; they did, and the Aussies got burned.

Another reason to have short-term contracts is that your Chinese counterpart's employees probably won't be around for more than a year. The people you will work with—sales managers, engineers, and accountants—usually don't last too long in a Chinese SMB. Annual turnover rates in Chinese companies are very high, sometimes over 100 percent for companies with less than one hundred employees. Most of the turnover comes just after the Chinese Lunar New Year, in January or February, when employees collect their annual bonuses and take off for new, higher-paying jobs.

In one case in 2006, a European plastic-injection machinery company chose a Chinese distributor because of their strong engineering talent. They had five engineers educated in Germany, all of who spoke German and had previously worked at the European company's competitor. It was a match made in heaven: existing technical expertise, market familiarity and experience, and no translation or cultural issues.

The German CEO wanted to lock in a five-year exclusive contract with them. I fully understood the difficulty in finding such an ideal partner, as it took me over nine months to find them, but I strongly advised him to sign a twelve-month contract instead. I suggested they let some time pass and see how things went first before deciding on a full-blown marriage. I begged the CEO to at least include an escape clause that allowed him to void the contract if the five engineers left the company. "Or why not offer regional exclusivity so at least all of China is not lost if they fail?" I asked. "No, that wouldn't do," said the CEO. "We don't want to upset the relationship, and we don't have the time to train multiple partners."

Well, against my wishes, they signed. Sales were excellent for the first sixteen months. Then suddenly, without any warning, sales plummeted to nothing in the winter of 2007. At about that same time, the German headquarters started receiving phone calls from Chinese customers complaining about poor technical support. I intervened and found that all five engineers had left the company. Ultimately, we renegotiated and gave them exclusivity for the surrounding Shanghai area on the condition that they hire and train five new engineers. This mistake cost the Germans time, product orders, and more important, their reputation, which can be difficult to recover from in China.

Use Chinese Law Firms

It should come as no surprise that I recommend using Chinese law firms for any Chinese-related legal work. Western lawyers certainly cannot draft Chinese-language contracts, nor do they have familiarity with Chinese law. Besides having local legal expertise and knowing the Chinese culture and language, Chinese law firms, on average, charge much less than similar Western law practices. Law firms that in the United States charge $200 to $300 per hour may go for $50 to $150 per hour in China. On top of that, fees are negotiable, and they will accept project-based fees rather than hourly rates. And yes, these lawyers speak fluent English, graduated from the finest law schools in China (like Fudan or Tsinghua University), and worked as legal councils in international companies (such as Philips Electronics, Motorola, and General Electric). Many have done two- to three-year stints in the United States working in the China department of major international law firms.

Local law firms also have some additional advantages that foreigners don't normally think about. They have access to local city officials or central government ministries in case they need legal issues clarified or strings pulled. China's laws are vague and always changing, so local law firms need constant updating, whereas a foreign law firm may only obtain periodic reports. Local firms will draft both Chinese and English contracts, thereby eliminating any finger-pointing between the Western law office writing the English version and the Chinese office writing the Chinese one.

Chinese law offices will also have access to local tools to perform due diligence on companies, assets, and individuals. China lacks third-party organizations, like Dunn & Bradstreet, to check on a company's finances, but local lawyers can refer to state and city business registrations and filings, which are all in Chinese, for basic financial information.

Some of the public information, however, is questionable, as Chinese companies always have two books: one for public records and the real one, for themselves. Someday, local law firms will be able to tap into a state government and central bank-sponsored online system to check a company's credit and litigation history. This will take a few more years, but the system will only be in Chinese and will be accessible only to local, preapproved organizations and law firms.

Always use lawyers in the same city or at least the same province that your Chinese partner is located. If your partner is in Shenzhen, don't use a law firm in Shanghai or Beijing. A Beijing law firm will have little knowledge regarding Shenzhen business law. Much of the legal work in China (contract negotiations, due diligence, registrations, and so on) is done at the actual location you plan to do business in.

I once had a foreign SMB retain a Shanghai law firm to negotiate an asset-based deal with a Chengdu chemistry laboratory. The Shanghai lawyers traveled twelve times to Chengdu, increasing the total legal fees by 40 percent for the travel and additional hours. Some law firms claim to have branch offices in other cities, but you should make sure to actually visit these locations. Ask to see the legal registrations showing that the two offices are in fact related. Sometimes these so-called branch offices are just working as independent subcontractors. If that's the case, simply retain them directly, saving the 30 to 40 percent markup fees.

SMBs will also make the mistake of using their US-based law firms, which have law offices in China, for their Chinese legal work. These subsidiaries are not legally licensed in China to practice, as only local law firms are permitted to practice law and represent clients. In fact, any lawyers employed by foreign-based law firms do not actually have business licenses and thus cannot practice law in China. They cannot represent clients in court, sign documents as a legal representative, or technically give China-related legal advice. Any legal work they do is actually subcontracted to a local Chinese law firm. This adds costs. Foreign law offices don't like to tell their clients this, but they are no more than just middlemen. They essentially take a commission and pass the work on.

Enforcing a Court's Judgment

There is another vital reason for having a Chinese law firm. They will not only assist you in preparing a local contract or deciding whether a lawsuit is winnable in court, but maybe more important, they have the local expertise to judge whether a court's decision is actually enforceable. In the West, or at least in the United States, a court's judgment and enforcement of that judgment go hand in hand. There's no issue about whether a defendant will not follow through with a judge's decision. The courts will see to it that the decision handed down is strictly enforced. Not so in

China. Going to court is easy. Enforcing the court's decision is an altogether different matter.

Xu explains, "It's a time-consuming process if the defendant does not voluntarily pay. The courts are too busy, and the losing party will delay court proceedings, taking months or years to get compensation, if any. All in all, it's a tough road to get any money back."

Local lawyers will determine if a verdict is enforceable using several factors, including size and litigation history of the company being sued, the amount being sued for, and similar cases for precedent. The biggest determining factor will be the size of the company. Xu says, "If the defendant is a big company, then it should be no problem to receive compensation. We worry about individuals and small companies. They usually don't pay and [then] disappear, so for these cases we really have to evaluate the costs and the enforceability of any verdict."

I ran into a situation when one of my customers sent steel molds to a Shenzhen-based plastic-injection company to produce plastic kitchenware. The molds, valued at over $1 million, weighed many tons and were custom-made in Germany. About one year into the relationship, both parties became disgruntled. The American complained about quality issues, and the Chinese about unpaid invoices. I assisted my customer to find a new mold shop a few miles away and kindly asked the current molder to assist in the transfer of the molds. He refused.

We went to court in Shenzhen, forcing the molder to return the molds and pay for any unsettled damages. As expected, he did neither, and we went through the courts again to seek payment.

After some fourteen months, our lawyer told us that the shop owner had closed the company, left the premises with his four plastic-injection machines, and probably melted the molds and sold them as scrap metal.

Enforcing judgments on individuals is even tougher. They move, change identity, and vanish into thin air. Under no circumstances should a foreign SMB sign a contract with a Chinese individual with no ties to a registered company. Many overseas industrial component and equipment manufacturers sign consulting contracts with independent sales agents, who in turn find Chinese customers in exchange for commissions. I have seen cases in which unscrupulous representatives switched customers over to competing companies for higher commissions or stole thousands of dollars' worth of payments by cajoling customers to send them the funds. In all cases, the culprits simply disappeared. When we went to the police, they found that no such person or home address existed. But it didn't matter anyway. What were we to do if we caught them? They might get some jail time, but we'd certainly get no money back.

Think Differently

Now that we have some of the foundational contract details in place, I'll arm you with some tactics I use that can help you create a written contract that will provide a better working relationship with your Chinese partner. It took me a number of years to learn and test these principles, and I have found them to be very successful.

Win-Win Situation

For SMBs buying from China, the most important negotiated item is probably price. When negotiating, we are always taught to get the lowest price. I remember when I was purchasing electrical components while working at Philips Electronics in China, my manager told me to get the best price, and I inquired what that number might be. He said sarcastically (but with a hint of truth) that I would know when I exited the door and they called me back in.

But this strategy would eventually backfire, as the Chinese would find some way, usually at your expense, to lower their costs to match your asking price. The results are always a poorer-quality product. I call this phenomenon "quality degradation" because it's a slow process. The first couple of shipments always contain first-rate quality products. But somewhere down the road, never immediately, different materials will be used, fewer quality checks will be conducted, and, even more frightening, another cheaper factory will be contracted out to make the goods.

The toy industry was a victim of this game. On one end, the toy companies' quality managers insisted on high standards to ensure children's safety. On the other end, unbeknownst to the quality department, the toy companies' purchasing department beat the factories down to the most godforsaken, lowest humanly possible price. The factories could, of course, say no to the work, but they knew that competitors would easily take the job. Most factories have the motto, "Take the deal first, and worry about making money later."

And thousands of Chinese toy factories did exactly that. They took below-cost jobs and then sought ways to cut the bill of material. Shortcuts were taken like using lead paint, which dries faster and so reduces production costs and lead times, and substituting lead for more expensive metals like silver or nickel.

The lesson here: calculate production and material costs and never buy below those estimated prices. Western manufacturers will walk away from the table when buyers ask for ridiculous prices. Not the Chinese. Many will accept below-cost prices and then find ways to beat them, by hook or by crook, making the buyer the ultimate loser in the end. So know how much you want to pay and calculate a fair and honest profit for your Chinese partner.

For other issues, like delivery schedules, insurance, and shipping costs, estimate fair numbers based on common sense, logic, and industry experience. Giving your Chinese partner a fair deal will allow them to make some money and thus lessen the urge to cheat. Similarly, when selling to China, make sure a distributor or licensing partner has enough profits to make a comfortable and reasonable living. If not, this may lead to counterfeit products or pirated software. Make it a win-win situation.

This attitude is very counterintuitive to what Western businesspeople have always been trained to do—buy at the lowest possible price and sell at the highest possible price. I always get push back when proposing this nontraditional strategy. I remember making a proposal to a New Jersey–based lighting company that was outsourcing electronic ballasts and fixtures from China. They were experiencing high ballast-failure rates in the field, which meant high replacement costs. The labor costs to replace ballasts could be many times the cost of a single electronic ballast and could potentially put the lighting company out of business.

The lighting company was paying far below the bill of material costs. I told them it was impossible for any manufacturer, even a Chinese one, to make a half-decent electronic product at that price. So I recommended to them to raise the buying price, but on the condition that the Chinese use better, imported electronic components to improve quality. The quality manager understood my comments, but the import manager became totally disgusted with me. "You must be kidding me! It's not my job to raise prices. Why should we pay higher prices for them just to maintain minimum quality standards? They should be doing this regardless of what price we pay them. We aren't paying you consulting fees for stupid advice like that. They must be paying you to give advice like that. Get out of my office!"

Needless to say I didn't last too long with that company. It's difficult to ask anybody to actually negotiate for higher prices. Some get my reasoning behind it, but most don't. But I know from dozens of outsourcing projects that this strategy will pay dividends in the long run. You will still have relatively lower pricing but noticeably better quality, delivery times, and most important, a solid, reliable partner who is happy to work for you.

Self-Enforce Your Contracts

Any contract will have some conditions and terms that we entrust to our partner without proof or verification. For example, a buyer rightly assumes a syringe factory will conduct proper quality tests for a given sample size. The syringe factory will submit test data, and the buyer, unless provoked, should have no reason to suspect that the data was falsified. Everybody is innocent until proven guilty.

In China, though, it is better to assume that everybody is guilty until proven innocent. During negotiations, think of ways your Chinese partners could miss key processes, for example, skipping manufacturing steps, using unspecified raw materials, or mislabeling products. Besides accidental errors, analyze "mistakes" done on purpose, or in other words, the ways you can be cheated. Once all the techniques have been ferreted out, look to eliminate them either through additional measures in the contract or with actual physical corrections on the factory floor. Some methods have been to add third-party inspectors or to drop-ship raw materials to eliminate the use of cheaper substitutes. The process is tedious, time-consuming, and irritating. As I mentioned before, we don't like to think bad thoughts about our partners. It may seem self-defeating to want to work with someone who will do bad things, but in the long run, it will be better for you and your Chinese partner if you evaluate and try to circumvent every corruption possibility.

In one case, I instructed an American medical company purchasing syringes from China to thoroughly examine all the ways a Chinese syringe factory could make quality- and manufacturing-related errors, by accident or on purpose. On our factory visits, we negotiated the right to have surprise audits and quality checks performed by independent supply-chain inspectors. Further, the American company placed drop-ship orders directly with their foreign resin, silicone, steel, and paint suppliers to reduce the possibility of the Chinese using cheaper local materials. We allowed manufacturers to use some locally made components but insisted on verifying purchase orders and wire transfers. I even made calls to the local suppliers to match lot numbers with the shipments. Finally, finished goods were pulled off the trucks heading to the port and taken to a local lab for chemical and physical inspections. Nothing was left to chance. We thought we had foolproofed the complete process. Until one day.

We discovered that the owner had subcontracted some of the work to his brother's factory just across the street. "We did nothing wrong," replied the owner when questioned. "My brother's factory uses the same equipment and materials. Even the managers are the same. In fact, you would have never known the difference if you hadn't seen the boxes being carried across the street. I see no reason for the Americans to be so angry."

Technically, the owner was correct. We never specifically stated the work had to be done at that exact factory. We had missed a step; we didn't explicitly make clear that only one factory—the one we had inspected—must be used. But shouldn't it have been obvious? Not to this factory owner. He had followed our instructions word for word, but he lacked the foresight or sophistication to see the big picture: we wanted a previously inspected and controlled environment with no variables to corrupt the production and quality of the syringes. Ultimately, it was my fault. I shouldn't have expected the Chinese owner, someone of the Mao Generation, to consider our motives above his own.

The Big Picture

The last example shows that the Chinese sometimes just do things wrong by accident or unknowingly, or as I mentioned in chapter 1, they lack a fundamental understanding of the big picture. Depending on their backgrounds and experience, they may comprehend all the little things asked of them, but often they may not be able to put the pieces together to understand why they are doing them or what the end results are.

A personal experience illustrates my point. In 2004, I traveled to China with my father. We were on a tour bus traveling to

Xian to visit the Terracotta Warriors. The bus was filled with both Westerners and local Chinese. The tour guide passed out Kentucky Fried Chicken box lunches to all of us as we headed toward our next destination. As we were eating, Westerners picked the meat from the bones and then delicately placed them back in the boxes to discard later. The Chinese, however, rolled down the windows and nonchalantly flipped the bones out into the open air, some actually hitting pedestrians and bicyclists on the roadside. My father was furious; he stood up and scolded the locals in Chinese. "You should all be ashamed of yourselves, polluting your own country and allowing foreigners to laugh at you! Have some respect and stop trashing China."

The locals looked shocked at first, not expecting to be yelled at by an old Chinese man. Finally, after some mumbling, they all nodded their heads in agreement and, one by one, started putting the bones into their lunch boxes. One local Chinese woman even applauded and thanked my father for the lesson. "We don't want foreigners to look down on us. After all, we have been taken advantage of by foreigners for hundreds of years. We should show them who we really are."

My father sat back down beside me, and I could tell he was quite proud of himself. In some minute way, my father, an engineer and professor, felt he had done some good for his people and country. My father's speech set the way for at least these thirty Chinese passengers to never aimlessly pollute their motherland. Now he had only 1.3 billion more people to teach. I told my father I was impressed that our Chinese companions had actually understood his point. Unfortunately, I spoke too soon.

Moments later, a middle-aged Chinese mother and her teenage daughter finished their meals, put all the bones and used napkins into their boxes, and then opened the window and threw the boxes out, along with their empty cups and utensils. Within minutes, everybody else did the same, leaving my father and the foreign tourists in bewilderment again. The tourists blindly followed my father's instructions but did not comprehend the reason why they should not throw the bones. They didn't understand the bigger picture: that we should not pollute. Similarly, most Chinese businesspeople will follow, say, manufacturing instructions per a contract, but they may miss a step or two because they lack the understanding of why they are performing each task. They fail to understand the main purpose, the end result.

During contract negotiations, we often describe processes from step A to step C skipping step B because logic or intuition dictates that everybody already understands step B. But if they "don't get it," step B is not obvious. Not knowing the big picture results in not understanding the causes and effects of each step, so they may go from step A to step C, missing step B completely. Foreigners will then accuse the Chinese of cheating, but in reality, they didn't even know a step B existed.

Play Loosey-Goosey

In chapter 4, I discussed how the Chinese treat contracts as agreements that can be renegotiated later if faced with changing market conditions. Even though the contract period is, say, two years, a Chinese businessperson would have no qualms insisting on lower pricing or lower sales quotas, as if it were an unalienable right to ask for and get these demands. Foreign SMBs should handle contracts the same way. Forget the Western way of thinking that contracts must be honored at any cost throughout their entire lifespans. Instead, like the Chinese, make your contract a moving target that enables you to ask for changes as needed. Give yourself the same advantages that Chinese businesspeople award themselves. Don't get mad; get even.

I previously wrote about a Chinese software distributor wanting to renegotiate their contract with an American enterprise software developer. Before signing the distributor contract, the Americans had some reservations about granting exclusivity for all of China to an unknown company with only fifteen employees. Price was also a concern, as the distributor had requested very low pricing. Throughout the whole negotiation, I reminded my client that the terms could be altered at any time, even after the contract signing. If we later found a better partner or wanted to raise prices, we simply had to give a viable reason for our new course and demand the changes. The distributor wouldn't sue, couldn't retaliate, and would either give in or end our relationship. It was that simple.

In general, Chinese SMBs will accept contract changes as long as there are good business reasons to do so. Supply-demand changes, raw material shortages, human-resource issues, or different strategy directions are all valid justifications to ask for a new contract. Just don't be malicious in your intent. The Chinese respect good, solid business practices and know when it's time to give in a little, but they will not react well to an obvious malcontent. Be smart and don't go overboard when asking to renegotiate.

Once a Swedish customer of mine, an automotive component manufacturer, had an unfortunate incident with his Chinese distributor. After a mutually beneficial eight-year relationship, things turned sour overnight after the two parties had a few too many drinks. Jokes turned into sarcastic remarks, which later turned to outright insults. It became personal, and ego got in the way of what was previously a good thing. Making light of my past lessons on Chinese contracts, the Swedish manager demanded 40 percent higher prices, claiming higher material costs. The distributor wasn't dumb, though; they knew the material costs since most of them came from China—and why hadn't they gotten wind of these higher costs months before, through warnings as they had in the past? The Chinese distributor retaliated by commencing a public smear campaign against the Swedish manufacturer, which resulted in lost revenues, customers, and brand image.

Chapter 5 Summary

1. Even though Chinese contracts are far from being foolproof, you still need to have something in writing. It doesn't have to be anything fancy, but get an agreement on paper so you at least have a basic framework for the relationship.

2. When creating a basic Chinese contract, follow this general advice: use both English and Chinese languages; include an arbitration clause so if a suit is filed you don't have to go through the Chinese court system; keep the contract period short, preferably less than twelve months; and highlight the main issues—price, product specifications, sales quotas, and schedules—in a summary page.

3. Always use local Chinese law firms to draft Chinese contracts. They know the local legal climate, have access to local databases to perform due diligence on companies, and are generally cheaper than foreign lawyers. More importantly, they have experience handling disputes and can decide whether a case is worth taking to court.

4. Don't ever sign a contract with a Chinese individual. The risk that he or she will disappear in the end is too great.

5. Never trust that your Chinese partner will follow the contract terms and conditions. You must enforce the contract on your own. Look for ways a Chinese partner can cheat you, and then look for ways to eliminate those possibilities.

6. The Chinese sometimes are not purposely trying to cheat on a contract. Foreigners need to fill in the details as to why certain things are done a certain way. Toy manufacturers, for example, didn't understand the ramifications of using lead paint in toys. I blame these problems on the differences in financial, social, and educational levels between Western and Chinese businesspeople.

7. The Chinese will change contract terms to suit their needs. You should do the same.

Chapter 6
Negotiations: A Never-Ending Process

Sometimes, negotiating with the Chinese can be the most painful part of doing business in China. At least it is for me. And it's not just arguing over prices. Everything gets haggled about—from more product features and extended warranty periods to free shipping and better payment terms. In chapter 1, I discussed how building trust and group harmony were overplayed in China. Well, the negotiation styles of the Chinese prove my point. I understand we all want a better deal, but most businesspeople work for this within socially expected boundaries; we don't push these limits for fear of losing the bigger deal.

Not so for the Mao Generation Chinese. They seem to go after small issues as if they were a matter of life and death, without concern for the overall relationship. On top of that, they seem to have all the time in the world. They'll talk something to death or until foreigners lose their patience. I'm convinced this stalling tactic plays a part in their strategy, as they know that Westerners have deadlines to meet. Negotiation styles are also very different for Chinese SMBs compared to the large SOEs, and I'll explore the intricacies in dealing with both.

Haggling at Beijing's Silk Market

Negotiating with Chinese businesses parallels a visit to the many local shopping centers that cater to foreigners wanting to buy fake branded goods. In Beijing, I often frequent the Silk Market, where they sell anything from fake Armani suits, Calloway golf clubs, and Lego toys to pirated Windows 7 operating systems and Nintendo Game Boys. The place is an eight-story building with hundreds of small stalls, each about the size of a hotel bathroom. Each floor has its specialty; the first and second floors sell women's clothing, and the third floor hawks children's clothing and toys. Each stall tries to differentiate its goods by creatively laying and hanging their products to attract pedestrian traffic.

Young girls in their teens and twenties almost always work the stalls, and they are very effective. I equate their abilities in business and negotiating tactics to the best savvy Chinese business owners. In an instant, these girls can read you, judge you, and make a calculated guess as to how much you will pay for that fake Gucci bag or pair of True Religion jeans. You see, prices are not marked on the goods, and this is done purposely. The girls verbally quote you a price, and that number depends on the day's supply and demand, the time of day, and more important, their profiling of you. They'll quote a higher price to Americans and Western Europeans, who are perceived to be richer, than to people from poorer countries, such as Nigeria or Poland.

The haggling starts as soon as your eyes glance over the merchandise. She quotes some ridiculous price, and you come back at half that price. This goes back and forth many times. Eventually, it turns into a shouting match. If you are not careful, a fistfight may break out, but you come to your senses and walk away. But wait! She calls you back and finally gives in to your previously "absurdly low" counteroffer. If you don't turn around, she'll chase you down, forcing you to take the item. Most shoppers give in at this point. As you dole out the cash, you second-guess yourself. *Did I get a good deal, or was I ripped off?* I know these incidents are all in good fun and part of the "China experience," but they leave a sour taste in your mouth. Yes, I got what I wanted and the price I wanted, but it came after an emotional roller-coaster ride of anger, ridicule, disappointment, grief, and then finally confusion, all of which are the same feelings I go through during negotiations with Chinese companies.

It's the Culture

I believe haggling is part of the Chinese culture. Sportscasters often use the phrase, "You're not trying if you're not cheating." Similarly, "You're not Chinese if you're not haggling." It's in the blood.

I enjoy visiting the early-morning vegetable and wet markets in the small and secondary cities throughout China. They open before dawn, which is perfect for me, as I'm usually jet-lagged during the first few days of a China business trip. I highly recommend that tourists and businesspeople alike visit these local markets. They give you a taste of old China as you see farmers hauling their fresh produce on bikes and homemakers carefully selecting live fish or chicken for that night's meal. And once dinner has been chosen, the unlucky animals are slaughtered right in front of your eyes. You can hear the bantering back and forth between buyers and sellers: "This chicken's wings are broken—I want a discount," or "These fish come from a special river, so I can't go any lower."

In these small towns, anything locally made, produced, or grown doesn't have a price. Any transaction involving money must be accompanied by a five-minute haggle. I walked into a restaurant about an hour north of Yangzhou with our driver who was from the area. That day's dishes were scribbled on a chalkboard. As we ordered, our driver and waitress started arguing in their local dialect. After five minutes of this, the driver got 30 percent off the chalkboard prices. I was impressed.

I remember when I was twelve years old and going grocery shopping in Chinatown with my grandmother. We went there two or three times a week, as she always insisted on fresh meats and fish for the next days' meals. Now my grandmother had been living in America for about twenty years already, but I guess old habits never die. She would haggle with the butcher over inflated prices for oxtails, thinking it might get her a discount. It never worked, though the butcher sometimes slipped in a few extra slabs. Next, we visited the produce section, and she'd haggle with the produce manager, insisting that the string beans were too small and smelly. And finally, at the checkout counter came the usual ritual of complaining how good a customer she was and that she should get some freebees. It never happened except for an occasional double bagging by a bag boy who felt sorry for her. My grandmother couldn't help herself; haggling was ingrained in her. Like breathing, it was instinctive—a part of her soul.

Countering the Haggle

Haggling Is a Good Sign
If you see your Chinese counterparts haggling, that's a good sign. It means you are close or already at their expected price points;

they are now just trying to squeeze you for more. Just like in the shopping stalls, the girls won't even talk to you if your offer was not already a reasonable one. Even though I know the deal is done, I usually suggest giving in a little. This allows for some face-saving for the Chinese.

So how much should you give in? Pick a few of the most important issues for your partner—margins, lead times, warranties—and meet them halfway, while budging only a little on the other less important items. For the most part, this should appease them. But please note that my recommendations are only guidelines, as each negotiation is unique; weigh all the options before deciding.

Silence Is a Bad Sign

When I see frowns or hear silence or sidebar meetings, then I worry. It means an impasse exists, and it's not worth haggling; the salesgirls aren't calling you back on your price proposal. Another telltale signal is when Chinese say, "Let's discuss this matter later" or "We'll consider your view and get back to you." They are setting aside the tougher issues for a later date, realizing that trouble may lie ahead. The Chinese want to keep moving forward, making progress while leaving showstopper issues until the end. Make a note of these points in your head and be prepared for some roadblocks.

This example best describes how to handle these situations. I was negotiating with a Chinese auto equipment distributor on behalf of a small, Michigan-based manufacturer of liquid-dispensing equipment. After four months of on-and-off haggling, we settled the easy issues and were heading out to China for our fourth and hopefully last visit before signing the contract.

The Chinese, as usual, left the two most difficult two issues for the last round. First, they wanted the right to use Chinese-made spare parts since they were cheaper and cut lead times in half. This had been brought up four months before, but the president had made it clear that under no circumstances would he allow another manufacturer to make the company's branded parts. This was a deal breaker. As usual, the Chinese huddled and suggested leaving the matter to the last meeting. We agreed.

The second issue was just as polarizing. We were only going to allow the Chinese to sell to domestic automobile manufacturers, as we already had existing relationships with the European and American automakers. The plan was for us to set up our own subsidiary company in China to sell directly to our existing customers, such as Ford and BMW. The Chinese demanded the whole market, including foreign manufacturers. Again, taking the recommendations from the Chinese, the issue was postponed until the end of negotiations.

The final meeting ended in complete failure. Neither side was willing to budge. For the Chinese, using Chinese spare parts more than doubled their net margins. Ego got in the way of the second issue. They weren't happy covering just a portion of the market and didn't want to be told whom they could sell to. But there was no way we were going to share our direct customers, whom we'd wooed for over thirty years.

Solve the Tough Issues First

This failed business venture occurred early in my consulting career, and I was just as shocked and upset about the outcome as my customer. It was an eye-opening experience for me. I had wasted my client's time and money, and worst of all, I had left them high and dry without a China strategy.

I handle these situations very differently today. I won't ever leave major issues until later, especially deal-breaking matters. To be polite, I accept delaying the talks to a later date, say, tomorrow, but not weeks or months later. If these things can't be settled now, they won't be settled later, so you should get them out on the table immediately. Whatever happens, so be it.

Also, some issues like pricing have a middle ground. I want to sell at $100, and you want to buy at $50, so we can comprise at $75. Other business matters, such as exclusivity or product specifications, have no middle ground. You either have exclusivity or you don't. You either use Chinese-made parts or you don't.

In my example, if price were the final issue, I'm sure my client would have comprised, but the issues were far greater, risking both my client's quality and reputation. This old and proud company from Flint, Michigan, would have preferred to declare bankruptcy before allowing a third party to manufacture its branded parts. The issue was not negotiable. I should have known this and brought it up earlier with the Chinese.

Negotiating with State-Owned Enterprises (SOEs)

The key to knowing how to counter Chinese negotiation tactics is to understand your counterpart's vital issues. What do they deem to be most important? At first thought, this seems obvious. Business is business no matter what country you are in, so aren't price and profit the only things that count? Not in China. What's important to a Chinese company largely depends on their ownership. Privately held enterprises will more or less think along the same lines as Western companies. But SOEs are a different animal completely, and even among government companies, it's essential to know whether they are owned by the local or the central government.

To understand SOEs, we have to know what makes them tick, who runs these companies, and where they want to go. In the past, profits were of little concern, as they had unlimited capital resources from the central government. During Chairman Mao's time, government companies, or factories as most were at that time, served as welfare houses meant only to feed and house the local citizens.

Things are different now, as sales and profitability are definitely priorities. When China went from a central, planned economy to today's pseudo free economy, government companies no longer had a free lunch and had to begin to act more like privatized companies, making good products at good prices.

But state companies still have remnants of the past. Upper-management positions are almost always filled with appointed government officials. They are professional politicians, not businesspeople. Their personal interests are tied to the local and central government ministries. An aircraft component manufacturer, for example, might be headed by a government official from the Ministry of Transport. Such an official might have aspirations to return to politics and become a deputy member of the National People's Congress or to lead one of the many department ministries in Beijing.

City- or province-owned companies have civic duties toward their municipalities or province. The company leaders, often city mayors or vice mayors, direct the companies to serve the local areas' economic needs. These orders are often in conflict with a company's profits, core competence, or strategy. City-owned companies often go into totally different industries, such as a cement manufacturer forced to manufacture steel nails or a glass-making factory converted to make lightbulbs. Again, these are business decisions made by nonbusinesspeople, which usually leads to trouble.

However, some municipal decisions are sound. Take the city of Shenzhen, just across the Hong Kong border. The politicians there have directed and served their city well, making it one of the world's largest manufacturing hubs for textiles and building materials in the past and for electronics, telecommunications products, and contract manufacturing today.

The city has specifically pinpointed telecommunications as one of its core industries, and this is why it's the headquarters for two of the world's largest telecommunications equipment manufacturers, Huawei and ZTE. This is a more difficult task than you would think. To develop an industry from scratch, you not only need a core competence, but surrounding infrastructure as well. This includes a university to produce engineers to work at ZTE and Huawei, electronic manufacturers to make the components for telecommunications systems, and logistics companies to move and ship the products.

They Want Your Technology

Obtaining technology is another key driver for SOEs. Many lack the skill sets, experience, and time to develop technology on their own, so they find other means to bring it in. The quickest way is to work out a technology transfer with foreign companies. When China opened up business to the West in the 1970s, technology transfers through joint ventures were the only way large conglomerates like General Electric or Philips Electronics could break into China. Today, SMBs are also very active in technology-transfer deals. This is both good and bad. The good is that it allows many more foreign companies access to China's markets. The bad is that SMBs lack the sophistication and experience in knowing what to transfer, how to transfer, and what negative repercussions and risks may unfold. Many are only concerned about short-term profits and just don't take the time to think things through.

I seldom recommend "sharing" your technology to a joint venture. After all, you're giving away your core competencies and the foundation of what made your company a success. It's equivalent to loaning your engineers to another company. SOEs have a habit of improving on your technology, leaving their once strategically important foreigner alone in the dust. I actually believe this happens more to SMBs than to larger foreign multinationals. Large corporations are extra careful; they have dozens of lawyers and local experts handling the technology exchange. The Chinese are also careful not to annoy their multinational partners—by blatantly stealing technology—for fear of any negative publicity. Even with this said, some multinationals have made mistakes, for example, Siemens with its high-speed rail and Motorola and Cisco with their telecommunication technologies.

We Just Never Learn

To get a piece of the market, MNOs today are still willing to "share" their technologies with the Chinese. The Chinese are in the midst of designing and producing commercial aircrafts that will compete with Boeing's 737-800 series and Airbus's A320 aircraft and have solicited many MNOs to join them in their efforts: Rockwell Collins will supply the navigation systems, Honeywell International will handle the wheels and brakes, GE Aviation is building the avionics, and Parker Aerospace will supply the flight controls. There's nothing wrong with selling aviation technology, but the Chinese government forces the MNOs to form joint ventures with SOEs. Chinese and Western engineers will jointly research, design, and build new composite materials, engines, and avionics using Western intellectual property. The multinationals repeatedly contend that they have ways to protect their intellectual property, but I just can't see how when Chinese scientists and engineers are acting as principals in the development of these new technologies. We just don't learn from the past.

Similarly, SMBs act just as recklessly, if not more so, with their decisions regarding technology-transfer deals. I've had to hold back many American SMBs from giving away technology to potential Chinese suitors. SMBs often bark back at me, "Dealing with these SOEs is like working with the government; they have money and name brand, and they won't do anything illegal. There's no way the Chinese government will steal my technology."

I'm not saying they will steal your technology, but they may alter or improve upon it, resulting in newer and better technologies that they will claim as theirs. Hence, problems arise. Who owns the new technology? This becomes a "your word versus mine" issue in the Chinese courts, and once in the courts, there's little chance of winning. Remember, the SOEs and judicial courts are essentially all one and the same. And even if you do win a judgment, how much will you have lost in legal costs, time, and motivation to continue to do business in China? I know it's hard to say no to these huge SOEs, especially when they are promising hundreds of thousands, if not millions, of dollars in exchange for some circuit boards or source code. It's free money for a market you would have difficulty entering on your own. But saying no is still the right thing to do.

A Germany Company's Experience

One of my customers, a small, high-end German manufacturer of plastic-injection machines, faced technology-transfer problems in China. In 1995, they were approached by an SOE that manufactured similar machines but for the low-end market, making consumer goods like toys and shampoo bottles. They wanted a higher-quality machine to offer to the more profitable, high-end manufacturers in the aviation, medical, and telecommunication sectors.

At first, the Germans proposed a distributorship to the Chinese company whereby the injection machines would be manufactured in Germany and resold in China by the SOE. As usual, the haggling went on forever, with the two sides going back and forth on pricing, exclusivity, and annual quotas. Just when we thought we had a deal, one of the executives changed his mind, and we started all over again. We were deadlocked after two months.

Both companies took a few weeks off to rethink. Then one day, out of the blue, our partners had a new idea: Why not manufacture the German-designed injection machines in China using cheap Chinese labor and parts, thus avoiding import duties, long lead times, and shipping costs? In exchange, the Chinese were willing to pay a licensing fee. As it turned out, these fees were equal to the gross margins the Germans would have made selling the machines from Germany. Boy, what a great idea! A win-win situation.

This made great sense to the Germans, even better than the original distributorship they had planned. This new strategy required no capital investments, as they would use their partner's manufacturing facilities, which were already staffed with trained engineers and support staff. The Chinese estimated that in only thirty-six months they could capture 20 to 25 percent of the high-end plastic-injection market share while offering a European-style machine at 20 percent lower costs than those of their nearest European competitor.

This made sense to me too, except for one small caveat: the Chinese required the raw software codes that controlled the equipment, as all the graphical user interfaces had to be recoded into Chinese language. The codes were also required for maintenance and repair work. The software was essentially the heart and soul of the machinery—and the company. It had cost the Germans millions of dollars to develop. The Chinese, once they had the codes, could easily install it in their branded machines. Add some German training and some research and development (R&D), and the Chinese would be self-sufficient. The Germans would be left behind with an empty bag, wondering where all their technology, profits, and once-proud company had gone.

I argued vehemently with the Germans about this deal, but they absolutely wanted to move forward. I gave in. My motto is that the customer is always right, so against my better judgment, I proceeded to assist them. I still remember the day of the signing ceremony. It was a glorious day. The city's mayor was present. The Germans were thrilled, and Chinese company executives were bubbling with joy. Why not? After all, they had just closed the biggest heist of all time, and it was all legal. I don't know exactly what has happened since, but I do know the German company has not made any significant inroads in China nor are they present at the many plastics-related trade shows in China. The Chinese injection manufacturer, however, is doing excellently in both the Chinese and, until recently, European markets. They must have improved their technology.

Protecting Your Technology

So now it is clear that under no circumstances should an SMB risk its intellectual property trying to sell to China or even outsource from China. Here's an overview of the ways SMBs can protect their core technologies while, at the same time, not sacrificing any sales opportunities.

Work with Distributors

I advise my clients not to partner with their competitors whenever possible. A telecommunications equipment manufacturer, for example, should not partner with Huawei or ZTE, nor should a nano-material solar cell producer partner with Suntech Power Holdings or China Sunergy, two of the world's largest solar cell producers. Having these large Chinese companies as customers is encouraged if you are just selling them products like you would any customer. But this is seldom the case. Chinese MNOs typically integrate or embed other companies' products into their systems, requiring engineering work, training, and data sharing. Foreign companies will then send engineers to China with source codes, circuit schematics, and computer-aided diagrams. Soon after, the relationship evolves into joint-development work.

Seek out Chinese distributors selling similar products. These companies have just as much technical, selling, and market knowledge as a manufacturer. In fact, they may have better relations with end users since they are selling direct to them. Distributors will almost never develop their own products. They're making too much money to risk their existing relationships with their manufacturing partners, and most actually do not have the skill sets to copy a product. They specialize in logistics, customer relationships, and maintenance, and lack engineering and production skills. They are in the business of selling, not engineering or producing.

The only drawback to having distributors is that they are usually regionally based. A Beijing-based distributor will have customers and offices only in northern China, and circumstances will be similar with a Shanghai- or Shenzhen-based company. So instead of dealing with one large manufacturing partner, several distributors will need to be found and managed, which creates more work for an SMB with limited resources. But for me, it's a no-brainer to work with multiple partners who, at least, have no intention of wanting my technology.

If distributors cannot be found, then partner with manufacturers in the same industry that produce different but complementary products. I introduced a European power tool company to a Chinese nail and screw manufacturer who wanted to leverage their name brand. On another occasion, a Chinese manufacturer of residential air conditioners was looking to expand into the industrial market; cooling systems for factories require different technologies and products, so I felt comfortable introducing an American cooling tower manufacturer to them.

If No Other Choice
In some cases it's just impossible to find a partner except for another manufacturer in the exact same industry. I've seen this in the biomedical and medical industries, where the instruments are so specialized that only competing manufacturers possess the talents and experience to sell, market, and maintain the products. Further, in some industries the end users are accustomed to working with manufacturers directly, so no distributors exist.

When these situations arise, I recommended working with several smaller, city- or provincial-owned partners rather than signing up with one large state-owned or privately held enterprise. This minimizes risk in several areas. For one, any potential intellectual property theft will be limited to that region where the partner is located. Second, there's always a better chance for legal recourse against a city- or province-owned SOE than a private one, as I discussed in chapter 5. Lastly, these smaller SOEs may not have the necessary resources to reverse engineer complicated and advanced intellectual property. Remember, it takes an lot of manpower, time, and money to learn the insides of a computer chip or examine the details of several million lines of computer code.

Offer Older Technologies
Another viable solution is to offer older technologies, one or two generations behind, rather than the latest and greatest, thus

limiting a company's intellectual property exposure. At worst, older technologies are compromised while preserving current state-of-the-art technologies. This strategy works particularly well in China's medical industry, where many hospitals and municipalities are several generations behind the curve. Smaller hospitals in rural China are still using ultrasound machines made in the 1980s. They simply cannot afford the best equipment, so instead, when they upgrade they purchase used, older-generation machines made in the 1990s and early 2000s. Similar situations exist in the automation manufacturing, information technology, and mining industries.

Negotiating with Chinese SMBs

Dealing with Chinese SMBs is a whole lot easier. They share similar goals as Western companies, and those mostly involve making money. They don't have complicated, hidden agendas like the SOEs do. As long as there's money to be made, they will always meet you halfway. The only qualm I have with Chinese SMBs is that the haggling, mostly about money, goes on well after the contract has been signed. It's a continuous process.

Leave Some Wiggle Room

The key to countering these seemingly unlimited price demands is to know it will happen and to prepare for it during the negotiation phase. Here is a strategy I often use. Take your rock-bottom selling price and add 50 percent to it for your entry point. Hopefully, depending upon your haggling skills, you can keep the final price about 25 percent above the original rock-bottom price. This gives you another 20 to 25 percent to play with when your Chinese partner comes begging for additional discounts.

This strategy sometimes doesn't work, so I go to an alternate plan. If my consulting client agrees, I'll have a private back-office discussion with the Chinese, a kind of heart-to-heart talk from one Chinese businessperson to another. I'll apologize, saying that my clients are foreigners so they don't understand the market conditions in China. I'll then imply that I have the influence to change pricing on a case-by-case basis once we start really selling to China so they don't have to worry about the contract price—they should just accept it and move on. This "inside information" usually puts them at ease. I know my comments are an invitation for them to haggle, but I'm of the opinion that they will do it regardless. This just gives them confidence that the "final price" is not actually the final price.

The Buck Stops Here

Large Chinese corporations, like their Western counterparts, have excessive bureaucratic decision-making processes. Not so for Chinese SMBs. The owner decides everything. Even the smallest of details, such as where to eat for dinner or the colors of a company banner, are decided by the owner. On one occasion, I even saw line workers march into an owner's office complaining about the cafeteria food.

Not having the owner at your meeting is a bad sign. It shows a lack of respect. After all, you have traveled halfway around the world, and the boss doesn't have the decency to spend some time with you. It also means your business just isn't that important. The owner is handling other things while the lower-level managers are serving as hosts. To save you some face, the owner may nonchalantly show up for dinner or karaoke in the evening. When these situations come up, I'll brush the business off and move on to bigger and better things. We are obviously not wanted there.

It's imperative that you always deal directly with a Chinese SMB's owner. Having face time allows you to get to know the owner, which provides insight into how the company operates. An owner who pays attention to details will run a tight ship: coming to work early and leaving late, watching the employees like a hawk, and making sure the day-to-day stuff is done on time and correctly. Foreigners should try to work with these types of owners. Conversely, stay away from an owner who seems unfamiliar with the company details. Such an owner rarely comes to work, preferring to sleep late or play golf. This lack of leadership leads to internal corruption, high turnover rates, and poor revenue.

Dealing directly with the owner also saves time. Owners can make decisions on the spot. You can get a lot done in a day when an owner is at your side. I recall one meeting with a distributor where all the key Chinese managers were present, but we could get very little done. Our questions went unanswered, and crucial issues were deferred. We were talking to a wall. Things totally changed when the owner walked in; he instructed his subordinates to get us everything we asked for. Managers started sharing information, people started making calls, and communication went a lot more smoothly. We accomplished more work in two hours than we had in the previous six.

Chapter 6 Summary

1. The Chinese will haggle everything to death. It's part of the culture.

2. When your Chinese counterparts are haggling, it's a good sign. It shows you are close to a deal. It's a bad sign when they are quiet and unresponsive. This indicates that terms are too far apart.

3. Chinese businesspeople will try to push difficult issues to the end of the negotiation process. Rather, bring them to the forefront and get the hard stuff resolved first.

4. It's sometimes difficult to negotiate with SOEs, as they have different priorities than privately held companies. It's not just about money for the SOEs.

5. Obtaining foreign technologies is a key driver for Chinese SOEs. Never compromise your technology and intellectual properties. Foreigners have gotten burned in the past, giving away high-speed rail and telecommunications technologies.

6. Negotiating with Chinese SMBs is much easier. Their motives are simple: money.

7. When negotiating with a Chinese SMB, always deal with the owner directly. The owner makes the final decisions. The lower-level managers are just messengers who yield little or no decision-making power.

Chapter 7

Selling to China: Answer Four Questions

In the past, only MNOs had opportunities to sell products and services to China. Heavy import duties, cumbersome banking regulations, bribery-happy government officials, and just a simple lack of basic knowledge about China prevented SMBs from cracking the country. Not today. Though still not a free-market economy, China has opened its doors to almost all comers. The keys are to know what products and services to offer and how to sell using a new set of rules.

Selling to China is like selling anywhere else except it has a few twists and turns. It's analogous to playing chess; but in China pawns can move horizontally as well as vertically, and kings can jump two spaces instead of one. Those of us who went to business school learned about the four Ps: product, price, place, and promotion. They still apply in China but with minor changes and variables we don't normally think of in the West. In China, intellectual property laws and enforcement affect product, labor costs lower price, drastic differences between suburban and rural lifestyles alter place, and language and everyday habits modify promotion.

Most SMBs follow the same strategies for China that they have used successfully in other foreign countries. At trade shows, I often meet SMB owners who balk at my services, claiming that since they have tackled South America, Eastern Europe, or Japan, China should be no different. I don't even try to convince them. They think what they think, and I know what I know. It's the businesspeople who have gone to China and failed who realize they need some outside assistance. As they say, ignorance is bliss.

This chapter describes the four basic questions that SMBs must ask themselves to determine whether their products or services will sell in China. Chapter 8 will focus on market-research methods, and in chapter 9, ways to sell in China—partnering or going it alone—will be examined. These three chapters combined should arm you with all the tools needed to make a successful venture into China.

Are Your Products or Services Right for China?

I ask these simple but often neglected questions when examining whether a product or service will have success in China:

- ○ Do your products or services have at least 25 percent in cost savings or have a nine-to-twelve-month payback period for your customers?

- ○ Do your products or services *not* have local competitors? Can they *not* be easily pirated?

- ○ Do your products or services have the China sales potential to make up 20 to 25 percent of your total revenue within five to seven years?

○ Do your products or services have a technological advancement that saves or improves lives, reduces energy consumption, or serves the present policies of the central government?

Try your best to answer these questions even though most of them require knowledge and experience in China. For some, the answers will be intuitive, and no additional research will be necessary. Others may require you to seek assistance from China experts, examine competitors' positions in China, or actually conduct market studies in China, which I will discuss in the next chapter.

Chart 7.1 examines some of the products and services that my clients introduced to China. As you can see, more yes answers means a greater chance for success in China. I won't take a consulting job unless the business can answer yes to at least three out of the four questions; anything less would make for a difficult challenge. I know other consulting companies (including some very big ones) that will take any SMB's money and promise great success and fortune. "How can you go wrong?" they rhetorically ask, explaining that almost anything and everything will sell to a country of over 1.3 billion people.

On the contrary, very few industrial or consumer-related items actually do well in China; this is mostly because just about everything already exists in China—or at least can easily be copied—at half the price. So take the time to do your homework before making the plunge; and most of all, look at your products objectively (a most difficult task for some SMB owners) and answer the questions as honestly as you possibly can.

Chart 7.1 Answering the Four Questions

Products/Services	Question 1: At least 25 percent in cost savings or less than twelve-month payback for customer?	Question 2: Products and services have no local competitors and are not easily pirated?	Question 3: Potential to represent 25 percent of total sales in five to seven years?	Question 4: Advance technology?	Actual Results of Introducing Product/Service to China
Avionics Equipment	Not applicable, as cost is not an issue for customers.	Yes, it will take China many years to develop its own technologies.	Yes, China is building its own commercial aircrafts that will compete with the likes of Boeing and Airbus.	Yes, the Chinese FAA prefers using already-established equipment.	Successful, all China-made aircrafts will use foreign avionics.
Vision Inspection Systems	No, payback is four to five years.	Yes, the software is difficult to copy or pirate.	No, not enough factories are willing to invest.	Yes, software will take years to develop.	Failed miserably, human eyes are cheaper.
Plastic-Injection Machines	Yes, machines are faster and provide for better quality, resulting in cost savings.	No, the technology can easily be copied.	Yes, China is the world's largest manufacturing country.	No, the Chinese developed its own technology in a matter of months.	Not very successful, machines were reverse-engineered.
Servomotors	Yes, less downtime.	Yes, intricate details and advanced software make piracy difficult.	Yes, many customers exist in China.	Yes, experience is needed to make high-quality motors.	Successful, especially for wind turbines.

	Yes, seeds yield more and better crops.	Yes, the Chinese are very weak in this field.	Yes, China needs to feed its 1.3 billion people.	Yes, it would take decades for the Chinese to come up to speed.	Very successful, China is suffering from food shortages.
Genetically Modified Seeds					
Electromechanical Liquid Medicine Dispensers	No, it is cheaper to do by hand.	No, it is a simple mechanical device that is easy to copy.	No, too costly.	No, it contains simple mechanical parts.	Failed, manufacturer dumped finished goods to scrap metal dealers.
US-Style Wedding Planning Services	Not applicable.	No, too many local competitors and locals can easily copy service.	No.	No, this is a service-related industry.	Failed, could not compete with locals.

Payback Period

With a calculator and industry-related data like labor rates and fuel costs in hand, I meticulously punch out payback analyses for promising foreign equipment, such as energy-saving cooling towers, automated assembly lines for disposable shavers, newfangled computer-aided laser cutting machines, and computer-aided design software. Unfortunately, most don't make the cut, having payback periods of well over four years. That's not to say a market does not exist for these longer-payback items; larger SOEs or MNO subsidiaries may have an interest, as they have longer-term business outlooks. But foreign SMBs are mostly looking to sell to other Chinese SMBs, and they just don't have the appetite for high-capital, long-payback investments.

Vision inspection systems are one example of an industrial success in the United States and Europe that has made little impact in China. These systems are high-resolution, high-speed cameras installed throughout a production line to catch faulty products and processes. They are popular for very critical components and products in the medical and semiconductor industries.

When I first started consulting in 2001, I was approached by a producer of vision inspection systems that wanted to expand into China's huge manufacturing industry. I thought the system made sense: it replaced manual labor, reduced bad product, and cut production downtime. I approached medical and electronics factories in China but was consistently laughed out of sales meetings. No Chinese factory was going to pay a hundred thousand dollars to replace a few girls working for two or three dollars an hour. Things are quite different now, with labor rates increasing dramatically, so these vision systems may yet have a chance.

Servomotors continue to sell very well in China. They are small, miniature motors used to run machinery needing accurate and consistent power output. Textile machines, for example, run on many of these finely tuned motors, needed for precision weaving and spinning thread. Less than a decade ago, German servomotors were two to three times more expensive than Chinese-made ones but had paybacks of six months due to reduced machine downtime and faster throughputs. Payback periods are even better today, as most of the foreign servomotor manufacturers now produce in China.

Pirating and Competition

You must absolutely make sure that your products cannot be copied in China. Legal protection through trademarks or patents is *not* a remedy. There must be a foolproof method that ensures that your product cannot be physically copied, pirated, or altered. Without these protections, don't even bother trying to sell to China. In fact, you could risk your existing sales outside of China, as the Chinese will find ways to penetrate international markets with pirated products.

A friend of mine produced boogie boards (soft, plastic miniature surfboards that young children use to surf at the beach) and wanted to introduce them to China's coastal cities. He found an exclusive distributor, spent hundreds of thousands of dollars in marketing, and did well for six months before his distributor copied the product and sold them under a different brand name at half the price. Soon after, other plastics manufacturers copied the boards, which soon made their way across the Pacific to Hawaii and the US mainland, forcing my friend into bankruptcy.

Never Compete on Price

Along the same lines, don't go to China if competent, local competitors already exist, and don't think you can make your product cheaper. The Chinese are experts in copying and making things less expensive. Many Western companies have used the low-margin strategy to try to gain market share in China; all have failed. Never underestimate the tenacity, competitiveness, and most of all, endurance for pain of the Chinese. The Mao Generation came from the low of lows; poverty made them tougher than we could ever be. They have nothing to lose and certainly won't let foreigners win on their home soil.

On top of all this, a foreign SMB's cost structure will always be higher than that of local Chinese companies. We bring expatriates, retain Western lawyers and accounting firms, and yes, hire overpaid consultants like me. There's also a hidden cost that foreigners are unaware of. We abide by Chinese laws when hiring local labor, paying taxes and duties, and repatriating funds. In comparison, many Mao Generation types cheat on taxes, pay less than the government-established labor rates, and bribe customs officials when exporting finished products or importing components and raw material.

Your China Business in Five to Seven Years

SMB owners are usually confused when I pose the question as to whether their China sales will be able to reach 20 to 25 percent of their total revenue within five to seven years. They usually answer, "What's wrong with just reaching 10 or 15 percent of total sales? Wouldn't you consider that successful?" The short answer is no, but it depends on the specific industry. If margins are abnormally high, then maybe 10 percent is fine; or if an industry has little or no organic growth, then going to China for small percentage gains sounds like a good plan. These are the exceptions.

For normal industries with 5 to 10 percent net margins and with revenue growing at about 3 to 7 percent domestically, I see no reason to go to China unless the sales potential will make a great and everlasting impact on the total business. The reason is simple: too much sweat is required to succeed in China—so make it worth your while. By now you know the hard work required to go to China; it will be a formidable task, draining financial and human resources, as well as being an emotional roller coaster. A new strategy has to be in place with new partners, different marketing plans, and possibly even new products. This big effort better have a big payoff. Why do it unless it becomes a major part of your total revenue stream? I know my "25 percent in five years" plan is subjective and each SMB has its own ideas as to what constitutes a big number. The main purpose in asking this question is to make businesspeople think about their long-term China strategy. Don't ever go to China thinking you can make a quick buck. Where do you want to be in five years, and is it worth the undertaking to reach that goal?

Advance Technologies

The last question as to whether a product or service has a technological advantage is self-explanatory. Chinese hospitals want to save more lives with better medical technology, and Chinese consumers will pay more for 3-D televisions. The Chinese government will, at almost any cost, find ways to reduce pesticides in the nation's water supply. In manufacturing, an example I've come across is laser cutting equipment that produced cleaner cut lines, thus increasing the quality of finished products, which could then be sold for higher prices. China is also actively seeking disruptive, game-changing green technologies (smart grid, biofuels, high-energy batteries, and many others) and will gladly pay more to reduce their dependency on fossil fuels.

Foreign companies in the aviation industry clearly have a technology advantage in China. This especially applies to aviation electronics or avionics, as companies like Honeywell and Rockwell Collins are light-years ahead of the Chinese. China's commercial airline manufacturer, Commercial Aircraft Corporation of China Limited (COMAC) is using 100 percent foreign-made electronics in its new C919 regional jet, which it hopes to sell worldwide by the next decade. COMAC would prefer to use locally made electronics, but it would take them too much money and time to get up to speed.

Further, a US Federal Aviation Administrator (FAA) in Beijing told me it would be highly unlikely that the FAA would approve any Chinese-made avionics equipment, thus also creating artificial barriers to entry. He said, "The Chinese will not use homemade avionics in our generation. They lack the technology, and there's no way in hell the FAA or the European Aviation Safety Agency would approve first-generation electronics. At least, I won't be the one signing the approval papers." Similarly, many of the major systems and components—landing gear, fuel system, and hydraulics—are also foreign-made or at least are designed by foreign aircraft parts companies.

Internally, COMAC management has also emphasized the use of foreign-made electronics and systems. A COMAC general manager told me, "We want to reduce all the unknown variables in the building of this new aircraft, so we try not to use anything new, and stay with well-known suppliers. It would be silly for us to develop our own electronics at this time."

Similar opportunities exist in the health-care, biotechnology, nanotechnology, oil and gas exploration, alternative energy (but not solar energy), and semiconductor industries. The Chinese are new to these markets, lack experience and education, see great domestic growth opportunities, and more important, cannot obtain new technologies without foreign assistance.

Chapter 7 Summary

1. Answer my four questions to help determine whether your products or services will have success in China. Don't even think about going to China if you cannot answer yes to at least three of the four questions.

2. Question 1: Do your products or services have at least 25 percent in cost savings or have a nine-to-twelve-month payback period for your customers?

3. Question 2: Do your products or services *not* have local competitors? Can they *not* be easily pirated?

4. Question 3: Do your products or services have the China sales potential to make up 20 to 25 percent of your total revenue within five to seven years?

5. Question 4: Do your products or services have a technological advancement that saves or improves lives, reduces energy consumption, or serves the present policies of the central government?

Chapter 8
Selling to China: Market Study

Hopefully you have been able to give favorable answers to the four market-entry questions in the previous chapter. The next steps are to actually spend some money and go to China to validate your answers as well as to obtain market data so, in the event that the study reveals positive results, you can build your business action plan. In China, you will have the opportunity to meet all types of people and companies, but more importantly, the visit will allow you to experience firsthand China's hustling pace of business, witness real Chinese doing real business, and experience the many side quirks about China—none of which you can fully grasp from reading a book. I lose touch when I'm away from China for more than three months. I go back to my American ways of thinking and forget the many idiosyncrasies of China. Again, China is not difficult; it just has a different set of business rules, and we have to be in the game to know the game. So go to China, learn the rules, and watch the players play the game before taking the leap.

When doing these studies, I don't set any criteria on whom I want to meet or where I want to go in China. I'll meet anybody anywhere just so long as they are related to my client's business. I don't set any preconceived ideals on the market. I go in totally neutral; I ask a lot of questions and do a lot of listening, absorbing information like a sponge. Foreigners, especially Americans, often go to China to tell the Chinese what to do. In meetings, they do all the talking and information giving and act as if they know more about China than the Chinese do. Don't do this. Americans don't feel comfortable listening in meetings. It makes them feel uncomfortable, unintelligent. As an American I often fall into this same trap and have to remind myself to shut up in meetings. "Stop showing off and listen," I say to myself. The study, the trip, is about *obtaining* intelligence, not giving it away.

Trip Logistics

Any market-study trip, especially one to China, requires tedious planning and great attention to detail. Don't just call a few Chinese friends, set up a few appointments, or study the latest *Frommer's China* and think you are now ready to get on an airplane. The trip preparation is actually more time-consuming and laboring than the trip itself. The key is sweating out the details. In this chapter, I'll layout a typical game plan I use for my clients. When planned well, the China study will be a pleasant experience regardless of the outcome. But if planned poorly, you may never want to go back to China again.

How Long?

The length of these market-study trips is usually seven to ten working days, not counting weekends, allowing for twenty to twenty-eight meetings in at least three locations. Start off with the least important meetings and cities and slowly work up toward the most important ones; jet lag can make the first few days in

China tough, so you may not be on your game through the earlier meetings. Also, as the week progresses, you become more knowledgeable and experienced, which in turn will allow you to ask more intelligent questions for the more significant meetings.

Try to plan for three or four meetings a day. It sounds difficult, but with proper planning, it can be done. Hotels can recommend a local driver; if possible, go over the addresses and schedule with him a day or two before the meeting dates. Preparation like this will shave up to two hours off your travels, as many China offices and factories are difficult to get to. Traffic can be a mess as well, but an experienced driver can find the shortcuts and back roads.

The work day can be extended with dinner and lunch meetings. It's a little odd for a foreigner to ask the local host to dinner since it should go the other way, but with a little coaxing, they should be accommodating. Other ways to shave time off include conducting meetings at the hotel where you are staying, taking evening or red-eye flights, and politely declining invitations for meals.

Where?

I always suggest visiting two major cities like Shenzhen, Shanghai, or Beijing and one secondary or outlying city like Wenzhou, Shenyang, or Chengdu. The major cities will account for 70 to 80 percent of a foreign SMB's total China business, as most of the major distributors, factory sales offices, and trade shows will be located there. The second-tier cities, however, are on the rise and should not be overlooked. The central government has been pouring billions into them, which means more infrastructure investments, job creation, and business tax incentives as well as better education and higher standards of living. This will all bode well for foreign businesses to either set up shop or find customers and partners in these new territories.

Choosing which cities to visit is industry-dependent, as city and provincial governments try to attract investments in specific industries. This is equivalent to Silicon Valley promoting high-tech companies and Minneapolis-St. Paul luring medical and biotech-related firms. A recently formed "China medical city"—located in Taizhou, about three hours from Shanghai—plans to be China's largest pharmaceutical, biotech, and medical equipment development zone. Chengdu is now becoming one of China's commercial aviation development centers. In 2010 the municipality began laying groundwork for a high-tech aviation park that will house high-end aviation mold development and civil airplane repair companies.

Foreign SMBs in the automotive market must visit Shanghai—home to Ford Motor (China) Limited, Shanghai General Motors, and SAIC (Shanghai Automotive Industry Corporation), along with hundreds of other tier-1 and tier-2 suppliers. Dozens of other auto-related companies have ventured two to three hours from Shanghai in such places as Nanjing and Chengzhou. Besides eastern China, cities like Harbin and Tianjin are now booming, as international companies like Volkswagen are establishing assembly lines there. With that, infrastructure will follow with tier-1 and tier-2 suppliers.

The south, mostly in the Shenzhen area, has long been home to low-tech electronics manufacturing like circuit boards, toys, and consumer electronics. With the advent of Huawei and ZTE, the area has become a recent hotbed for telecommunications.

Foxconn Technology, a major supplier to Apple, Hewlett-Packard, and other consumer electronics companies, has literally set up its own town within Shenzhen, employing over four hundred thousand workers. There are a smattering of medical equipment, auto electronics, and high-tech name brands in Shenzhen, but it's hardly worth the effort to go there for any other industries besides telecommunications and low-tech manufacturing.

Think Twice before Going to Beijing

Be cautious about visiting Beijing. It's a great place to go for Beijing duck and the Great Wall, but not so much for business. Beijing, like Washington, DC, consists mostly of government-related offices, SOE headquarters, and politicians. If business requires meeting them, then by all means go. But for the most part, Chinese companies don't have real, working operations there. Some do, such as Ericsson, Siemens, and Mercedes-Benz; but those are the exceptions, and they are mostly there because they were early entrants to China, arriving when it was deemed a necessity to be close to the politicians who decided your fate. That's not the case today.

In reality, corporate Beijing offices serve only as showcases to their customers. They are typically located in one of those new, gaudy skyscrapers in the Chaoyang district, home to foreign embassies and lavish expatriate residences. The employees working here are pencil pushers, accountants, human-resource and marketing managers—not who you want to meet to gather intelligence. They can provide macro-related information, which is nice for PowerPoint presentations to boards, but they lack the essentials needed to make life-and-death business decisions. Any relevant market study must consist of micro-related information like pricing, competitor product specifications, and customer names and contacts. To get the details, meet with the rank and file: the workers and managers running the day-to-day activities (sales managers, operations staff, and engineers); they are all at the factories, sales offices, and operation centers far from Beijing.

I once took an aviation client to Beijing to meet with the Aviation Industry Corporation of China (AVIC). This SOE is a holding company that manages dozens of commercial aircraft-related subsidiaries. These subsidiary companies are located throughout China and develop, test, and manufacture anything related to commercial aircrafts, such as wings, fuselages, and nose cones. My client develops test equipment to detect structural damage on aircrafts and wanted to meet specifically with the fuselage group that day. We ended up wasting the whole day meeting with pencil pushers, accountants, and human-resource and marketing managers. Dinner with AVIC's managers was even worse; they were all politicians who were more concerned about their political careers than detecting cracks on an aircraft wing.

Communicating with Your Contacts

Most of the communication with your contacts will be made through e-mails. E-mails are a good starting point, but never make it the last means of communication before your visit. Your messages will probably go through several departments and translations before getting to the exact person you want to meet. Even though your Chinese counterpart may confirm back in writing and everything may seem to be in order, have a Chinese-speaking person call to confirm whatever needs to be confirmed. And don't just do it once; make another call a week before you leave for China, as well as another a day or two before the actual meeting. It's most painful to have traveled to some secondary city many hours away from the nearest airport only to find out that your Chinese counterparts forgot about the meeting or don't have the right people assembled.

Another reason to have a phone call is to test English-speaking abilities. Many foreigners assume their Chinese counterparts speak English because their written English is excellent—only to realize they can't speak a lick when face-to-face. Most younger, educated Chinese can write and read English without any problems, but some either lack the ability or are too embarrassed to speak English. Chinese high schools and universities put more emphasis on teaching written English so students can pass the TOEFL (Test of English as a Foreign Language). Also, speaking in a foreign language requires practice, and most Chinese have little opportunity to mingle with foreigners. As discussed in chapter 3, bring a translator, or better yet a businessperson who speaks Chinese and knows your business.

Finding Contacts

Plan for a variety of meetings divided among potential customers, partners, and competitors; trade show events; foreign and local companies; and government entities, if applicable. And for each category, meet both large and small organizations as well as private and state-owned ones so you get the full landscape of your industry from top to bottom.

My initial investigation always starts with the US Department of Commerce (DOC). They are a wealth of information that most businesses are not aware of, and their services are relatively inexpensive. The DOC's purpose is to promote and expand

American products and companies in foreign countries, especially large ones like China. They have offices in Shanghai, Beijing, Shenzhen, Shenyang, and Guangzhou and employ English-speaking locals who specialize in most of the major industries, including the aviation, automotive, medical, and oil and gas industries.

Gold Key Service

American companies should participate in the DOC's Gold Key Service, a program that matches local Chinese companies with foreign SMBs in the same industry. The local DOC representative will not only set up meetings but will also accompany you to them. The cost for the service is about $500 per city.

Another advantage of working with the DOC is that they can set up meetings with the large SOEs like Bank of China, China Unicom, or China Petroleum. As big as these companies are, they would never dare snub a US government agency's request for a meeting, for fear of getting their employees' US visa applications rejected. Fortunately for us, they don't realize the DOC doesn't issue visas. Besides getting appointments, the DOC can pinpoint the exact department and person you want to meet, which can be a daunting task when navigating through the dozens of divisions and tens of thousands of employees.

In one incident, the Guangzhou DOC office set up a meeting for my clients at Huawei, now the largest telecommunications equipment manufacturer in the world. Upon our arrival at the main gate, an entourage of Huawei executives (and photographers flashing away) greeted us; we were given a gift and treated to a company tour while being escorted by one of their senior vice presidents. After the meeting, Huawei treated us to an extravagant ten-course lunch. Besides the presidential welcome, we met the right people in the right departments, making the day a complete success. My compliments to the DOC.

The service does have some drawbacks. For one, they will not translate for you in meetings. Second, DOC representatives cannot give opinions about your business, any meetings, or strategies moving forward; they simply act as neutral parties throughout a visit. So they won't tell you if a meeting went well or not or which partner is better to work with. First-timers to China need professional advice, so it's recommended you bring someone along who can offer objective insight, analysis, and clarity to your meetings.

Hong Kong
The Hong Kong Trade Development Council is another source for contacts. Similar to the DOC, their objective is to promote Hong Kong's business advantages and persuade foreign companies to set up operations in Hong Kong. Hong Kong companies often have operations in China or maintain close ties with Chinese companies, so they can steer you in the right direction. At the very least, they know the local business climate for your industry.

Trade Shows
If possible, try to coordinate a China trip with a trade show. Everybody who is anybody is usually at these shows. They present a great opportunity to meet potential partners, spy on your competitors, and gather intelligence. And don't just go to Chinese shows; try the major shows in Japan, Hong Kong, and Singapore. The exhibiting Chinese companies take their English-speaking staff, so English won't be a problem.

At the Singapore Air Show some years back, we met key executives working for Chengdu Aircraft Industrial Company, Harbin Aircraft Industry Group, and Shenyang Liming Aero-Engine Group—all leading players in China's aircraft industry. At the show we secured contacts that later turned into key on-site meetings and eventually some actual business for my European aircraft parts manufacturer.

Local Universities

Chinese universities and government-owned research institutions are another source for contacts and meetings. University names in China usually denote their disciplines—Beijing Forestry University, China University of Geosciences, Tianjin Urban Construction Institute—so it's easy to find the one that matches your industry. Typically, these centers of higher learning are eager to meet foreign visitors and showcase their knowledge and contacts. For example, I once walked into a state-owned chemical research institute and was able to see scientists raising chickens and pigs in the chemical testing chambers.

Surprisingly, Chinese universities, like government ministries, have the power to form companies and profit from them, so they could potentially serve as business partners, customers, or distributors. I've met university professors who served as presidents of foreign joint ventures. These university companies often reside on campus, with employees working for both the school and company. In general, I don't recommend foreign SMBs partner with them. Chinese universities, like SOEs, can sometimes have skewed goals that involve power, politics, and corruption. So definitely meet with them to learn about your industry, find other contacts, and absorb the nuances and oddities of doing business in China, but steer away from any closer ties.

Competitors

With my client's permission, I sometimes call their competitors in China. It seems odd, but more often than not, they will agree to meet. For one, the Chinese subsidiaries of foreign parent companies are typically manned by local Chinese, who are often not aware of the rivalries that fester outside of China. Second, there's so much going on in China that competitors might see some synergies in working together.

When I was consulting for a large American company that manufactured industrial cooling towers, I managed to set up meetings with their Chinese and European competitors in China. The American company teamed up with a local competitor to supply them with high-end cooling towers, a product that was absent from their portfolio. In exchange, the Chinese manufacturer allowed the American company to utilize their national network of maintenance and servicing outlets. Although the two companies fight like dogs and cats in Europe and the States, in China, it was truly a match made in heaven.

Philips Lighting China and Siemens is another odd couple in China. They hardly ever work together outside of China, but they subcontract ballasts and other lighting products to one another in China. I think the main reason these relationships exist in China is because China is growing so fast that consumer-related and industrial-equipment manufacturers simply can't keep up with the high demand, so they often go to their competitors to fill the gaps. This should continue as China maintains its 7–10 percent annual growth rates.

Study Completed: Go or No Go?

Ideally, upon completion of the study, a go/no-go decision can be made. Based on my experience performing over fifty market studies, approximately a quarter of SMBs will validate the positive answers to the four questions and will move forward with their China expansion. Similarly, another quarter will concede that their products or services did not receive a passing grade on the four questions. To these SMBs, I say don't give up hope. China is constantly changing, so revisit China's potential again in two or three years. Many products that were not suitable just a few years ago, such as aircraft-related products and services, are now very applicable because of China's rising labor costs and its intention to be a dominant player in the commercial aircraft business.

Found Another Market

Another quarter of SMBs actually find new markets or uses for their products and services in China that they had never thought of before, so they need to go to China a second time to flush out any remaining unknowns. In 1995, I performed a study for Carley Lamps, a medical lamp manufacturer based in Torrance, California. We spent a majority of our time visiting distributors who specialized in selling medical-related products and end users like hospitals and clinics. We were turned away at every corner; there were simply too many low-tech lamp manufacturers in China. The market was happy with cheap lamps and wasn't interested in spending more for higher-quality, longer-lasting lamps. I was losing all hope until one distributor mentioned that his friend, a mining helmet manufacturer, was seeking better-quality, foreign-made lamps. I spoke to his friend by phone, and he told me that the central government was investing more money into better mining equipment. At that time, there had been a rash of mining accidents, which had killed hundreds of trapped miners.

Upon our return to the States, we regrouped. We later went to China again, but this time to visit coal mines and mining helmet suppliers and manufacturers. They were interested, and Carley was able to design and manufacture a double-filament lamp that met China's light output and footprint specifications. Carley had found a new market.

Just Can't Pull the Trigger
The remaining quarter of SMBs are the fence-sitters, who are still confused and undecided. Some had very productive trips, while others had mediocre ones that didn't reveal any definitive conclusions. But it doesn't matter; they simply can't make a decision. We could go to China ten times, and they still can't—or won't—make a decision.

Why can't they decide yes or no? Maybe they heard too many horror stories about China or they just can't commit to a big investment. Any way you put it, when businesses are undecided with all the facts in hand, it's a telltale sign that they are not ready to go to China. At this point, there is little a consultant like me can do but say, "Thank you for the business. Let's try again in two years."

Someone Needs to Step Up
Undecided SMBs typically have a management team that simply "follows the herd." No single executive wants to stick his or her neck out and take the blame, or kudos, for going to China. After all, why fix what's not broken? Let's just stay with the status quo and let another company fail in China.

Conversely, sometimes there's one individual in an SMB who believes that going to China is the right thing to do. This one influential insider could be anybody—an owner, a vice president, a chief engineer—who truly believes in China and is willing to risk his or her job on it. This person is rare and hard to find. But every once in a blue moon, I'll find this one crusader who is willing to gamble, to go against the consensus, and push that go button. I hope you can push it.

Here's a perfect example of what I mean. I took yet another American medical company, based just outside of Denver, to Wenzhou to outsource syringes. After visiting several factories for over a week, the four key decision makers—the quality, materials, logistics, and manufacturing vice presidents—felt very comfortable with outsourcing from one of the factories. They pored over pounds of quality documents, inspected dozens of injection machines, and watched the assembly processes for hours as millions of syringes rolled down the conveyer belts. Over dinner, all four unanimously agreed to tell their president, who was also the owner, in a conference call the next morning that they had no problems buying from China. After dinner, the logistics VP and I called it a night as the other three VPs went to the bar for some after-dinner drinks—and, apparently, for some further discussions about China as I later learned.

The following morning during the conference call, each person spoke up, giving their thoughts about China. The manufacturing VP was first to speak. "You know, I'm just not confident that these Chinese factories can do the job. The quality seems inconsistent at times." *What the hell is going on*, I thought to myself. *He just told me last night that he thought the factories had great quality systems.*

The quality VP was next. "I'm in total agreement. I don't like the Chinese-made injection machine they use, and they make all the molds by hand, which bothers me."

The materials VP also had negative comments about doing business in China. I was shocked and felt cheated, but could do nothing about it; I was only a consultant. The logistics VP was last to speak, and I was expecting some vindication from him since he hadn't been engaged in the side discussions from the night before. "I think we might be taking some big risks if we go with China. Maybe we should wait a year or two, when their quality improves."

I felt betrayed. How could they tell me how good these factories are one day, and the next, tell their president how awful they are? These were the same factories that many of my past clients passed with flying colors. I was especially irked by the logistics VP; he was supposed to be on my side.

After cooling off, I realized I was being overly critical of these four men. China was too foreign, too scary, and too risky for them. After all, this was their first visit here. They could hardly finish their first dinner in China because of the dead duck's head staring aimlessly at them. They weren't about to risk their jobs and livelihoods to save a few cents by buying syringes from a third-world country. It was just too bold of a move. It wasn't the time to be a hero.

Chapter 8 Summary

1. After successfully answering at least three out of the four questions, you are now ready to go to China to perform a market study. The market study should accomplish several goals. First, the information gathered should confirm your positive answers to the four questions. Second, it will serve as the basis for your action plans—who will you partner with, how will you sell, and what price will you sell at? Third, it's an opportunity to see firsthand what China is all about. Seeing is believing.

2. A China trip should be about ten working days. You should visit three cities and conduct at least twenty meetings.

3. Finding Chinese contacts can be difficult, but here are some methods I use on a routine basis. The US Department of Commerce and the Hong Kong government have services dedicated to assisting American and other foreign SMBs with selling their products and services to China. Also, try to attend Chinese and other Asian trade shows related to your industry and visit universities that engage in research and development for your industry. And always make a point to visit your competitors, both international and Chinese ones; you will be surprised by what you can learn at these meetings.

4. After completion of the study, one of four likely conclusions will be made. SMBs will decide to go to China; to forego China; to go back to China to perform a second market study; or to "fence sit," not having the gumption to make a decision either way.

Chapter 9
Selling to China: Distributors

If you are reading this chapter, I hope it's because you have performed a successful market study and are now ready to take the next step. You have cleared a big hurdle and made one of the toughest business decisions you will ever make. Unfortunately, it doesn't get any easier as we move into the action-planning stages of actually setting up in China. Much of how to set up in China depends on the types of products and services to be sold to China, but I would venture that 80 percent of SMBs will fall into the general approach I'm about to describe—one I have recommended successfully to many of my clients.

Initially, I always take a conservative approach to China, not wanting to spend too much money. Start slow and build up the business progressively and then, only after testing the waters, begin to make bigger investments and risks. Chart 10.1 illustrates the seven ways to sell to China, from the most conservative to the most aggressive plans. I urge readers to analyze which approach best suits your company and industry. Finding distributors has always been my favorite starting point, since it's basically the most cost-efficient. Distributors can be found by word of mouth, visiting trade shows, or identifying disgruntled partners working for competitors.

Selecting Partners

When selecting and interviewing distributors, seeing is believing, so always visit them at their offices. Don't make brash decisions based on phone calls or quick meetings at hotels. See their operations, talk to the sales staff, go on customer visits, and inspect warehouses. If they distribute other products, query their partners to measure their satisfaction and sales revenues. The process is similar to finding a distributor in the United States, but with one caveat: don't just take their word—verify everything with your own eyes. Take nothing for granted.

I recall one incident when I was seeking computer hardware distributors for Kingston Technology. I met the owner of a Shenzhen computer distribution company, Mr. Zhang, at a small local hotel in the outskirts of Shenzhen, which was rarely visited by foreigners. Over lunch, he bragged about how big his company was—offices in fifteen cities, over one hundred employees, relations with all the big-name computer companies. He went on to say that with his contacts and experience, he could turn Kingston's annual China sales into a $30 million business in less than twenty-four months.

Keep in mind that, in the early nineties, Kingston was a small, no-name memory manufacturer competing with the likes of IBM, Samsung, and Toshiba. Nobody had heard of Kingston, but this man was promising to make it into a household name. It sounded too good to be true, so upon my return to California, I asked to speak by phone to several of Mr. Zhang's subsidiary offices and to the big-name vendors he was representing.

A call was set up with another Mr. Zhang from their Beijing office, and then a second call with another Mr. Zhang from their Chengdu office, and two more followed—all with Mr. Zhangs. Now, Zhang is a popular surname, but not *that* popular! The vendor calls were strange too; their names were not Zhang, but in the background I heard babies crying or grandmas screaming that dinner was ready.

It was a no-brainer. I was being bamboozled. It turned out that Mr. Zhang was a one-man operation working out of his house. The Mr. Zhangs I had spoken to were all his relatives, and his "vendors" were just friends and family. I eventually did find distributors for Kingston but only after visiting ten cities on two separate China trips. I made it a point to visit every distributor's offices, no matter how far off the beaten track. Boy, did I learn my lesson.

No Exclusivity

I always prefer working with several regional distributors over just one exclusive partner for all of China. I know in some cases, as with large industrial equipment where sales projects and customers are few, it makes sense to have one partner. But for products that have more mass appeal, with hundreds of customers in many locations, always go with at least three to four regional partners. You can allow each partner exclusive rights in their region; so, for example, a Beijing distributor will have rights for northeastern China, and a Shanghai partner will have exclusivity in the east.

For foreign SMBs without local offices or employees in China to watch over the market, the best watchdogs are distributors who compete and bad-mouth each other. Each one will keep the others in check. I'll be warned if somebody pirates products, slashes prices below our agreed-upon plan, or sells outside of China. No question, this creates channel conflict and price wars, but I'd rather deal with those sorts of problems than have a single distributor run wild, doing God knows what with my product.

In my greener days, I granted a Shanghai company exclusivity for all of China to distribute electrical components (capacitors, resistors, and voltage regulators) for my American client. Unbeknownst to me, fake components started showing up in the market. We only found out sixteen months later when a customer sent a box of burnt capacitors back to California for fault analysis. The units were labeled with our brand, but they weren't produced in our factories. More and more bad components started coming in, and soon we had a big problem on our hands. Piracy ruined my client's reputation, created a financial liability, and destroyed any future chance of succeeding in China. I vowed never to offer exclusivity again.

Channel Conflict

The channel will be complicated and confusing, but rather than fear it, expect the mass fray and learn how to deal with chaos. The key is flexibility. Set the rules in the contract but allow wiggle room in the day-to-day operations. Let the little things slide; lose the small battles, but win the big ones. I'll allow distributors to take advantage of me or temporarily cheat on petty items. It's part of the give-and-take that goes on between buyers and sellers. Somewhere down the road, however, I want payback, and it may come in larger orders or higher margins.

One of my software clients had trouble managing their four Chinese distributors. Each of the partners had exclusivity in their region and was strictly prohibited from selling elsewhere. Each bad-mouthed the others, claiming they were ruining the market by establishing cutthroat pricing, pirating software, and selling beyond their territories. I listened daily to all the attacks and was always on the side of the complainer. "Yes, you are right—that other partner is bad. I'll talk to them and stop it," I usually commented. But in reality, it would have been impossible to control the day-to-day activities halfway around the world, and I would have gone crazy trying. I would allow a distributor to steal small deals, or cross sell in other regions just so long as everybody at the end of the year made their fair share. I only stepped in and mediated when matters got out of hand or were outrageously unfair. There was one situation when the northeastern China distributor stole a large deal from the southern China partner after they had spent many months wining and dining the government customer. I broke my silence and gave the deal back to the southern Chinese company and abruptly fired the northeastern distributor. I took swift, decisive action when needed and set an example that major offenses would not be tolerated.

In another example, I knew one of the software distributors was also selling our competitor's product, which was strictly forbidden. But I allowed it just so long as they maintained their annual sales quotas. On one occasion, I learned of a big government software contract and wanted it badly. I gently suggested to the distribution company's owner that he should tender our software or else he might suffer dire consequences if our competitor won the deal. Needless to say, we won the contract. I give up nickels and dimes for the bigger prizes.

Contracts

As readers know by now, I'm not keen on Chinese contracts, and I never put much effort into preparing or maintaining them. I'm comfortable scratching out a simple term sheet and signing it. What's more important is to look the distributor in the eyes and make sure he or she verbally agrees to the most important issues.

Foreign SMBs should never give payment terms, especially in the beginning stages of a relationship. Too many SMBs allow for thirty-day terms, only to get burned. I've seen $200,000 worth of merchandise sent over only for the partner to never be heard from again. As I wrote previously, tens of thousands of dollars, let alone a few hundred thousand dollars, is worth reneging on a relationship in China. The scammer can live happily ever after in the countryside.

You will undoubtedly need to use my "wiggle room" pricing strategy (chapter 6) when negotiating price with Chinese distributors. Remember to always add 50 percent to your rock-bottom price. Even after the contract is signed, they'll come back and hit you up for more, "My sales costs are too high. I had to bribe some purchasing managers. The competitors are bidding lower." Regardless of the reason, you can now afford the discounts. Of course, you give them a hard time, think it over, tell them they owe you in the future, and then begrudgingly acquiesce to their demands. This game will be played over and over again, but you have already factored it in and now have a win-win situation. The distributor "wins," thinking they got a better deal, and you win, selling at hopefully well above your rock-bottom price.

Sales quotas are a must for any Chinese distributor contract. Quotas are like prodding sticks; they keep distributors alert, anxious, and uneasy. With quotas, distributors are acutely aware they could be let go in a few months' time—and you let them know that, often. It also keeps street pricing at bay, forcing distributors to maintain lower pricing to sell more quantities. Without quotas, they'll sell less at higher margins. It's a good short-term negotiation tool for short-term-minded Chinese distributors. Fight fire with fire.

Stocking orders go hand in hand with quotas. An order at the start of a relationship levels the playing field for you and the distributor; both players have skin in the game. There's no reason for foreign partners to bear all the costs while Chinese distributors, having no financial risk, pick and choose what they want to sell. More importantly, your partner won't cut and run with tens of thousands of dollars' worth of inventory sitting in the warehouse. A stocking order also shows that the distributor has confidence in your product and that it will definitely sell in China; Chinese companies won't buy what they can't sell. This, in turn, gives you added incentive to invest and support your partner.

Short-Term Thinking

Chances are your Chinese distributors will also be SMBs, all having similar characteristics: an office located in one of the major cities, a staff that speaks little or no English, no more than ten employees, always seemingly short on cash, and day-to-day operations being managed by the owner. But the most important trait I want to focus on is their propensity for shortsighted thinking. This can be both good and bad for you. The advantages are that they focus on the matter at hand—selling your products and services as quickly and efficiently as they can. You need this in the beginning stages, when doubt exists for your China business. They know the competitors, have access to customers, and deliver quick sales, thus assuring your short-term success and survival.

For the bad, they lack a long-term perspective. And this doesn't mean five or even two years from now—they don't even know what's coming in the six months. Owners are too concentrated on this month's profits, spending all their time haggling with you, and they do not put enough effort into considering longer-term issues like how to grow the business. This daily grind may make you wonder what is to come six months in the future—when they can't even think past two weeks! Again, this goes back to the discussion in earlier chapters of the ever-changing political and economic conditions in China. They change so fast that business owners know they have to earn money today, since there may be no tomorrow. So to some extent they shouldn't be faulted; they are just a by-product of the environment they live in.

But this myopic thinking often stunts growth. You want bigger things next year, while your partner is happy with short-term profits, not wanting to "waste" any of it on advertising, traveling, and other potential growth opportunities. At this point, you probably have outgrown your partner. In the beginning, they were excellent; they started the business for you and got things off the ground. But after a year or two, you want to see growth and market share. At this time, you'll need to do one of two things: either find bigger, more well-known distributors or start your own operations in China.

Chapter 9 Summary

1. Using Chinese distributors is a safe and conservative approach for first-timers going to China. The initial investments are low, and having a partner buys you time as you learn more about doing business in China.

2. Always interview prospective distributors face-to-face, at their offices. Visit their warehouses, go on sales calls with them, and talk to other partners they represent. Failure to do this will result in scam artists getting the best of you.

3. Chinese distributors will ask for exclusivity. Never give it to them. Seek a mix of distributors spread out across China. Having multiple distributors will secure a competitive playing field and control pricing and pirating.

4. Sign short-term contracts with distributors. Don't give them payment terms. Force them to purchase an initial stocking order, and negotiate annual—if not quarterly—quotas.

5. Distributor use is a good short-term strategy, but it will eventually stunt your growth. When it's time—and you will know when—make bigger investments into China and seek other opportunities.

Chapter 10
Selling to China: WOFEs and JVs

WOFE is short for Wholly Owned Foreign Enterprise and is essentially a limited liability company (LLC) registered in China. It's a Chinese legal entity that must follow the rules and regulations of Chinese business law, no exceptions. A WOFE acts as a legally independent, stand-alone company from its foreign parent. Similar to a US registered company, WOFEs pay taxes, hire employees, issue invoices, and collect revenue.

However, a few caveats exist. The Chinese government has forced foreign companies to register their local Chinese companies under this WOFE umbrella, something that local Chinese companies are exempt from, thereby segregating them into a special "foreign" category. WOFEs don't share equal rights with domestic Chinese companies. They cannot independently engage in one of the seven government-regulated industries (medical/pharmaceutical, telecommunications, banking, entertainment/media, aviation, automotive, and energy industries); have different regulations with respect to registered capital deposits, withdrawals, and repatriation of funds; and must submit financial forecasts and business plans as part of the registration process. A good Chinese business lawyer can recite the many other differences. To make matters worse, WOFE laws are not static; Beijing, like clockwork, makes changes to the WOFE laws every year, changes that depend heavily on the short-term business climate and temperament.

Reasons for a WOFE

A company will usually establish a WOFE for one of the following reasons: it outgrows its distribution channels and needs a more hands-on approach to its China activities, it requires local manufacturing, or it sells a niche or highly specialized product that distributors or other third parties cannot handle. After a year or two in China with consistent but not growing sales, an SMB may want to look beyond its shortsighted distributors and widen its customer base, market share, and sales revenue. The two choices are then to either find bigger and better distributors or establish a WOFE. Distributors with wider national coverage are rare; the best ones seem always to be regionally based entities serving local markets. A distributor in Tianjin (a city in northeast China), for example, will always know the local territory better than a national distributor based in Shanghai with only a field office in Tianjin.

With a WOFE, you can now go directly to end users or at least manage your existing sales channels better, provide local product support, and create brand awareness that you couldn't do before. After four years with distributors and good but stagnant sales revenue, my enterprise software client established a WOFE. We opened a small eight-hundred-square-foot office on the outskirts of Shenzhen, where most of our customers were located. The WOFE had a sales engineer, two direct sales people, and a marketing manager, along with an expatriate general manager. Employees from headquarters shuffled back and forth to train the Chinese in sales and marketing, troubleshooting, and accounting. No question things were tough in the beginning stages, as the WOFE mounted losses from higher-than-expected operating, marketing, and travel costs, and lower sales as we scaled back on distributors and took key accounts direct. Slowly but surely, the business turned around in two years, and soon after, sales increased due to bigger and newer accounts along with better brand awareness from local advertising. This is a success story that can be attributed to the WOFE establishment.

However, not all WOFEs can claim victory. Most fall short of expectations. In general, WOFEs, for both SMBs and multinationals, will lose money the first three years as companies learn the ropes. The most common mistake is underestimating the transition period from a start-up to becoming a fully independent, self-sustaining operation. Difficulties include WOFE registration delays, high employee turnover, longer employee training periods, insufficient headquarters support, export/import red tape, high travel costs, and localizing Western sales and marketing plans. Large corporations can bear the financial bleeding for three years, but SMBs typically bow out after two years. The pain is too much to bear.

The key to not failing is to not have such high expectations during the start-up phase. Expect to lose money, and plan for a rough road ahead. Conversely, expect things to get better. After the initial two to three years, you will have discovered most of the surprises, learned some good lessons, and resolved the language and cultural issues, allowing the WOFE to run smooth, clear, and in the black. This brings up a very important theme that I've tried to convey in my writing and which I have highlighted in my thirteen rules in the last chapter: think long-term but react short-term. Success in China has and will always be a long-term play. A business must have a minimum of a three- to five-year time horizon before it sees any windfalls. But while you are thinking long-term, don't make the mistake of maintaining the status quo in your sales, marketing, or other operational plans or actions. Keep the long-term plan intact (to be profitable after three to five years), while at the same time exhibiting flexibility to react or take new actions depending upon changing external factors, whether they are economic, political, legal, or environmental. In the short-term, don't be afraid to lower prices, alter product offerings, or modify advertising campaigns at a moment's notice. I guess this advice is akin to the story of the tortoise and the hare but with one exception: the hare, and not just the tortoise, has some pretty good traits we should emulate, at least when in China.

WOFE Registration

I'll save the gory details of the WOFE registration process, as it's basically a lot of paperwork and government filings. The key to a successful and timely WOFE filing is to find a good lawyer. Seek attorneys who are experienced in your industry, have filed many WOFE registrations, practice in the city in which the WOFE will be located, speak fluent English, and possess good hand-holding skills so they can take you step-by-step through the many cumbersome processes. A sign of a good law firm is that they will always end up waiting for you, rather than you waiting for them. An example of this is their paperwork will be completed but cannot be filed until you supply them with a myriad of documents that include a business plan, financial forecast, WOFE name, bank statements, proof of trademarks, and letters of incorporation.

Legal fees for the WOFE registration vary, but remember, you get what you pay for. Also, legal costs are higher for manufacturing WOFEs compared to sales-only ones. Additional paperwork, approvals, and studies are needed, such as environmental-impact studies, waste material declarations, and ministry-level applications. Using various Internet registration companies, a simple WOFE filing can cost as little as a few thousand dollars, but this route is not recommended. These companies are impersonal fly-by-night organizations that treat the whole process like a cookie-cutter operation. A shabby WOFE filing can cause delays by many months, even up to a year, negating any cost savings they offer.

Take a day or two out of your China business trip to interview two or three law firms. The cheapest ones will offer their WOFE registration services for between $3,000 and $10,000. These are usually local law firms, handling local Chinese SMB issues, that try to dabble in the expanding international legal trade. They do good work, but English communication as well as personal service can be problems, since they are probably used to handling rude and inconsiderate Chinese companies as clients. Their offices are also situated in hard-to-get-to places and in older, run-down buildings.

Go with middle-tier law firms situated in the better areas of town and in larger, newer buildings better suited for doing business with foreigners. The best way to find one is through word of mouth. Ask other companies who have done WOFEs for references. The major Chinese cities also have American Chamber of Commerce offices. Walk in and ask for a list of law firms that deal with international clients. These middle-tier law firms charge between $20,000 and $30,000, a fee which is negotiable, especially if you throw in other legal work, such as trademarks, patents, and annual government registrations. Don't go by hourly rates; rather, ask for a fixed package fee. The better law firms should comply. Higher-end law firms that typically handle larger multinationals can charge over $100,000 to handle a registration, but that's going overboard. In most cases, an SMB's WOFE registration will be relatively simple, especially if manufacturing is not involved.

Obtaining the business license takes three to four months, depending upon your industry and how efficient you are in getting documents and information to the lawyers. Once you receive the business license, you can now technically open a bank account, wire funds, sign an office lease, and hire employees. Your China business has begun.

Another piece of advice to adhere to when selecting a law firm for any purpose (WOFE registration, trademarks, patents, lawsuits, and so on) is to use China-based law firms. Only local, China-registered law firms can legally practice law and employ licensed local lawyers. Lawyers working in a foreign law firm actually do not have a license to practice law in China. The government will not issue a lawyer's license to Chinese lawyers working at these foreign firms. Few foreigners are aware of this, and even fewer foreign law firms inform their clients of this strange but true quirk. Let's say, for example, your US-based law firm has offices in Shanghai; they cannot actually practice law, represent you in court, or sign documents as your China legal representative. They can only advise you as a consultant. When they register a WOFE, they actually subcontract the work to a local Chinese law firm, and that is why these foreign offices sometimes charge outrageously high fees. They are just acting as middlemen.

The one drawback to using local law firms is that the legal concept of attorney-client privilege does not exist in China. So whatever information you give to your Chinese lawyers can and may be transferred, voluntarily or by force, to other authorities. Government agencies often coerce local law firms to hand over confidential client information or face suspension of their lawyer's license or even criminal charges. I wouldn't worry about this too much for the simple stuff—WOFE, patent, or trademark registrations—but do seek a Western law firm having experience in China if something more serious develops.

Location, Location

Choosing the location of your WOFE will be the single most important decision you make in determining the success or failure for your WOFE. Business owners get confused by the myriad of factors they must consider regarding the location. Some put emphasis on tax incentives given by local municipalities, while others are more concerned about the availability of local hires. Only one thing matters to me: proximity to customers.

China has not yet become a jet-setting nation. It's still relatively expensive for Chinese businesspeople to fly. China's urban per capita income was about $2,900 as reported in 2010 by China's National Bureau of Statistics. A round-trip flight from Beijing to Shenzhen conservatively costs about $400, which would be over 13 percent of an average Chinese salary. Compare that to the United States, where average per capita income in 2010 was about $39,000; a $400 round-trip airfare from Los Angeles to New York would constitute only 1 percent of the average American salary. I would venture to say only about 10 percent of the total Chinese population has traveled on an aircraft—a luxury reserved for business owners, top managers, and employees of multinational companies. These figures tell me that Chinese businesses, for the most part, buy products and services locally, thus making it vital for your business to be close to your customers.

Another reason to stay close to your customers is that Chinese business relations at the SMB level are still largely regionally based and quite discriminatory. Northern Chinese would prefer to do business with other northerners as would southern Chinese with southerners. The Shanghainese are especially prejudiced; they speak a dialect unintelligible to outsiders, eat heavily sweetened Chinese dishes, and consider themselves the prettiest, smartest, and purest breed of Hans. Regional bonding or cliques exists all over China, from Wenzhou in the south to Harbin in the north. I once met a Wenzhou leather factory owner who made it a point to only hire Wenzhou locals and buy his materials from other Wenzhou-owned companies. He told me he could always trust a Wenzhou person. I'm not sure about that, as my grandmother always told me not to trust people from Wenzhou! (She was from Tianjin.)

Besides the regional aspects, there are just plain practical reasons to be where your customers are. Chinese want to see the products they buy. Even in the Internet age, it's difficult for consumers to buy something via mail order or online without kicking the tires. For example, even though the product can be purchased online with one touch of a button, my software client's Chinese distributors must first download the software, package it into CDs, and then hand carry them to the customers. China is still basically a "pay and take" society.

Most of your China transactions will be conducted in cash. According to a China Central Television (China's state-owned television network) survey in 2007, only 20 percent of Chinese people own credit cards. Customers will come to your offices carrying thousands of dollars' worth of RMB in exchange for medical equipment, syringes, circuit boards, and anything else you can think of. A Beijing friend told me he once took $100,000 in cash to the local bank to pay for his apartment. On the way, he kept looking behind him to see if anybody was going to rob him.

In 2008, one of my clients, an environmental and reliability testing company based in Southern California, was confused about where to set up its China testing facilities. The company serves many vertical markets, including the automotive, aviation, and telecommunications sectors. We struggled and went back and forth trying to decide on the best China location. My client simply had too many customers in too many locations. China was building up the aviation industry in western cities like Chengdu and Xian. The surrounding Shanghai area had many automotive research and development centers along with manufacturing. Shenzhen had two flagship telecommunication customers—Huawei and ZTE—along with a plethora of smaller consumer electronics companies.

During the market study, I met with the major customers in diverse industries (Ford, Boeing, and Ericsson, just to name a few) and discovered that these customers not only wanted to see their components and systems being tested, but they also wanted to inspect the test equipment and setup, consult with our engineers on the test procedures, and perform failure analyses on broken parts. There was little chance they would send parts to other cities for testing. Shipping would be expensive, and many parts were just too big (for example, complete automobile transmissions and aircraft fuselage parts). On top of that, customers were rushed for time and favored labs that would pick up and drop off parts while performing tests in the evenings. Location was definitely their top priority when selecting a testing lab to work with.

Once we got this kind of feedback, it was a no-brainer. Regardless of the higher labor costs, electricity shortages, and traffic congestion, Pudong, a relatively new business development area in Shanghai, was the best choice, as it's within an hour's drive to over a hundred of the world's largest R&D centers for the automotive, commercial aviation, and telecommunications industries.

Reduce WOFE Expenses

As discussed earlier, most WOFEs will lose money their first three years due to underestimating costs, overestimating revenue forecasts, and having unrealistic time horizons. The cost overrides are usually due to high employee-turnover rates, domestic travel costs, expatriate travel, and sales and marketing localization. These costs cannot be avoided or mitigated. They are simply the cost a foreign company must pay to play in China. However, there are two things—headcount and salaries—that can tactfully be controlled to greatly affect the bottom line. And these cost savings aren't trivial given that paychecks can take up more than half of a WOFE's monthly operating costs.

Foreign companies typically seek Chinese employees with English fluency, engineering skills, and experience abroad. These job-seekers are highly sought after. Further, they don't want to work for no-name SMBs; rather, their goals are to work for IBM, Ford

Motor, or Apple Computer. If you hire one of these hotshots, for sure, they won't be around for long. They'll stay with you for a while, gain some experience, and then move on to better pastures. Save the frustrations and look for lower-qualified employees who possess potential. A two-year technical trade graduate can be trained to become a full-blown engineer, or a barely conversational English speaker can take courses to become fluent.

A manager for a small US engineering firm once asked me to fill a technical management position for their WOFE. The qualifications included the following: electrical engineering degree, ten to fifteen years engineering and management experience, English fluency, and overseas work experience. Not one candidate submitted a resume in our six-month search. The reason was simple: this potential candidate was already working at a large multinational firm, earning above-average wages, and serving as a mid- to high-level manager, so why would he or she want to take a step backward to work for a small WOFE with fewer responsibilities, a lower salary, and no brand recognition? We lowered our qualifications: minimum two-year technical trade degree, five years engineering experience, English proficiency, and no overseas work experience. Needless to say, we received dozens of resumes.

Many of the WOFE's supporting functions, such as accounting, payroll, human resources, and security, can be outsourced to small local agencies. These outsourcing specialists actually cater to WOFE start-ups, knowing that WOFEs lack sufficient resources and often don't yet have enough internal work to hire full-time employees. The best part of their services is their flexibility; fees start as low as $200 per month for handling basic accounting functions all the way up to $1,000 per month for more complicated tasks like writing human-resource handbooks or meeting local worker safety compliance. What's more is that they can be turned off or on each month depending upon your workload. The larger well-known companies like Ernst & Young and PricewaterhouseCoopers also provide these services, but they can be rather costly, sometimes even more expensive than hiring your own employees.

Another alternative is to start off your operations by hiring part-time employees. It's not recommended to use part-timers from the everyday workforce, as they are usually unemployable. There's a reason why they cannot find full-time work. Graduate students at local universities can fill in and are usually very keen to earn extra income. It's also somewhat prestigious for them to work at a foreign company. If accountants are needed, simply make a visit to the finance department of one of the many local universities or trade schools. The same can be done for part-time engineers, translators, or scientists.

College professors can also be hired on a part-time or consulting basis. When we set up a WOFE in Tianjin for a US automotive components company, we recruited the services of a Tianjin University mechanical engineering professor. We paid the professor the equivalent of about $15,000 as an annual salary (rather than spending over $40,000 plus benefits for a full-time, experienced engineer). Multiply that several times over, and it turns into substantial savings for any company, let alone an SMB struggling in the early stages. What's more, the professor was well connected with many automobile SOEs in northern China, so we used him for sales calls as well. He got us in the door with such companies as Beijing Automobile Works and Hafei in Harbin.

Hiring Employees

Most SMBs, when ready to hire, go to local headhunters. They are expensive, sometimes charging rates similar to those charged in the United States. Further, though they often find top candidates, these job seekers don't stay in any one place for more than two years. Headhunter-referred employees are always job-hopping. Chinese headhunting companies and their sales staff are also a rather shady bunch of characters. They are supposed to check references, confirm salary histories, and provide proof of education, but many are actually in cahoots with the candidates, working together to doctor up resumes and pull fast ones on companies. I have interviewed dozens of headhunter-recommended candidates only to find out later, after doing my own background investigation, that they were not college graduates or did not graduate from where they said they did, did not work where they said they did, and had provided references that were either nonexistent or turned out to be family members. These cheaters should have at least warned their uncles and aunts to expect a phone call from potential employers.

Finding employees by word of mouth has always been my best experience. Ask your friends and associates for recommendations. Given China's face-saving culture, they won't steer you wrong. This is why in China many family members work together at the same company. Existing employees won't jeopardize their jobs or reputations in recommending an inept relative. My former employer and consulting client, Kingston Technology, a California-based company with two Chinese American owners, still relies on word of mouth to hire their workforce in their Shanghai factory. "We are one big, happy family," says Kingston's president, John Tu. "We have best friends, aunts and uncles, sons and daughters, and whole clans of family working at Kingston China. It's the best way to hire employees, and they stay with us longer." It's harder to leave a company when one's workplace is essentially home. Just don't go overboard, such as having a manager approve his or her sister's expense accounts. That will lead to definite trouble.

Look also to hire locals who originate from the same city in which your WOFE is located. Transplants have no attachment to their current residence; they get homesick or will readily take on another job in another city for a few more bucks. Locals, on the other hand, are not apt to jump ship so quickly. They are more anchored at home with houses, friends, and families, and will stay with a local company at lower wages, preferring this stability over working at a company in another city that is offering more money.

Integrating the WOFE

Besides cost overruns, another reason why WOFEs fail is the lack of a cohesive and succinct integration between the China WOFE and its parent. This integration comes in many forms—training, communication, knowledge transfer—but the most important is in the transfer of the company culture or spirit; it's usually the lack of this that generates failure. SMB owners speak of the intangible qualities that have made their companies successful. Well, these same features are what will make the WOFE successful. The only way to do this is to have employees from headquarters sit and work with the local Chinese employees. The locals see what you do: how you act with customers, treat fellow colleagues, and handle adverse situations. Sending expatriates for extended periods of time can be expensive but is well worth the effort.

Philips Electronics made it a point to train its overseas managers, engineers, and sales staff with managers from Eindhoven, the Philips headquarters in the early nineties. Likewise, Chinese employees were sent to Eindhoven for extended training programs so they could be nurtured and learn the ways, traditions, and philosophies of Philips. Philips had a way of doing things, and it made sure all its employees, wherever they were, were doing them the same way.

As president of Kingston Japan in the late nineties, I brought new Japanese hires to Kingston's headquarters for hands-on training. There they learned what it meant to work at Kingston with its atmosphere of mutual respect, equality, and loyalty among its employees. To exemplify this, all employees, even the president himself, sat in open-air, cubicle-style desks. Said Tu, "Every employee from Japan [or] China to South America has to know exactly what our core beliefs are. Without this, we are nothing, no better than any of the other memory companies out there. Our values and passing those values to all our trusted employees is what makes us number one." The Japanese employees returned home thoroughly impressed with Kingston's business ethics. It's no wonder why Kingston Japan became one of the largest memory providers throughout Asia.

Joint Ventures—Never Do It!

In China, a joint venture (JV) behaves like any other company, having its own management, office, profit and loss statements, business directive, and products or services. The only difference is that the owners are typically two parent companies, one being a non-Chinese enterprise and the other a Chinese one. Each parent company puts in capital, intellectual property, human resources, and other things deemed valuable to the JV. In the 1970s and '80s, foreign companies wanting to set up shop in China were forced by the central government to form JVs with Chinese companies. To make matters worse, Chinese companies held majority share, giving them almost complete control. There was no way around it, so early China entrants like Philips Electronics, Coca Cola, and Volkswagen swallowed their pride and formed JVs to get a piece of the action.

Business conditions are better today. China only mandates foreign companies in the seven restricted industries I mentioned earlier to establish JVs. So, for example, Ford China is not fully owned by Ford America, nor are General Electric Aviation or Shanghai Roche Pharmaceutical fully owned by their foreign parent companies. They are all JVs with large Chinese SOEs. But companies in unrestricted industries (consumer goods, basic manufacturing equipment, and enterprise software, just to name a few) can freely do business in China—or I should say as freely as Beijing will allow them to. It's best to check with a Chinese law firm for updates on China's regulations governing the unrestricted industries, as changes occur frequently.

Almost every foreign SMB wanting to set up China operations asks me to find a JV partner. I can only guess they are reading out-of-date books about China that recommend doing JVs. I also believe China business experts in their late fifties and sixties, who are now either consultants or high-level managers, promote JVs as a successful entry strategy. After all, it was the only way into China thirty years ago for these older guys and gals.

Misinformed businesspeople wrongly assume that finding a JV partner reduces risks. Nothing could be further from the truth.

Working for Philips Lighting in China in the mid-1990s when they had dozens of JVs, I saw the pitfalls: corruption, distrust, disgruntled management, and lack of communication. Today, with relaxed business laws, most of the JVs have folded or have been bought out by their foreign partner. Now, as a consultant, I spend half my time resolving JV disputes. I see pain and regret in my customers' faces; they wish they had never even gone to China. The mistake was not going to China—it was being enticed into a seemingly no-risk venture. Going to China was the right choice; doing a JV was the wrong action plan.

I can't say this with any more passion: do not ever, under any circumstances, entertain or think about entering into a JV unless you absolutely have to. The risks simply outweigh any advantages. And any advantages from a JV can be duplicated in other less risky partnerships, such as licensing agreements or distributorships.

Paper Tiger

Let's examine the JV risks and rewards. The newly formed JV company will be based in China. Your partner company is China-based and China-registered. Chinese managers will run the company. All documents will be in Chinese. You get the picture: everything is Chinese except you. You, the foreign enterprise, are not in China. You don't understand Chinese law, language, or culture. Effectively, the Chinese parent is running the joint venture, leaving you as an innocent bystander. Yes, you have board seats, visit China regularly, engage in financial audits and so on, but you are not running the day-to-day activities. Foreign companies may exert "legal" control of the JV, but Chinese parent companies have actual or creative control. They usurp all power over management, employees, accounting, and sales, while patronizing their foreign partners, who thus become de facto paper tigers.

JVs create unlimited and unknown risks. You own an entity but, for all practical purposes, have little direct control over it. You can inquire about issues and ask people to do things, but it's all indirect access. You are many layers away from where the actual day-to-day grind takes place. They could be cooking the books, paying off government officials, or falsifying business receipts, and you would have no clue.

Pro-JV consultants argue that these corrupt behaviors could happen in a 100 percent foreign-owned WOFE as well. Yes, I agree, but they will happen much less frequently. A foreign company has a more direct say in what goes on with its WOFE. If, for example, a parent company wants to take a hard stance on unethical behavior, it can do so much more quickly and effectively in a WOFE than a JV. Many foreign companies send their human-resource managers to WOFEs to educate their employees about corruption and the Foreign Corrupt Practices Act. A general manager can set an example by firing employees who falsify expense reports or pay kickbacks to customers. Management actions are decisive, and the effects are immediate. Not so in a JV. It's hard to have this direct impact on a JV when everything filters through another partner. The same decisive orders that would have been taken in a WOFE will be toned down by the JV's board of directors and trickled down to the rank and file via a company-wide e-mail that no one will read.

British-Australian firm Rio Tinto, one of the world's largest mining companies, exemplifies the unknown risks involved in joint ventures. In 2009, Chinese officials arrested four Rio Tinto employees on charges of stealing trade secrets and taking bribes while working at Rio's Chinese JV company in China. One of the employees was a high-level manager, head of Rio Tinto's iron ore operations. Many Australian politicians insinuated that the arrests were in retaliation for Rio Tinto's snubbing of a Chinese SOE's offer to invest $19.5 billion in the company in exchange for a minority ownership stake. (It had been a very sensitive issue, as many Australians did not want a company owned by the Chinese state to have access to Australia's natural resources.)

Let's imagine that this incident had occurred in a Chinese JV in which I was the foreign partner. Because I have limited access to daily operations and cannot enforce Western business ethics, I have to accept the possibility that these allegations could be true, especially given China's recent wave of government-related corruption scandals. After the arrests, my Chinese partner might thwart my requests to investigate the allegations. Potentially, I might not be able to interview employees, audit internal reports, or speak to the police or government officials. Further, I could even be expelled from China as an accomplice to the alleged crimes. Effectively, I have become an innocent bystander, or I should say, a guilty bystander. I've been totally in the dark from beginning to end.

The Three-Headed Monster

JV supporters will also argue that JVs simplify doing business in China, since foreign companies are handing off local business decisions to experienced Chinese management teams. Again, nothing could be further from the truth. It only complicates matters, making things worse because of what I call the "three-headed monster" effect. Each of the three companies' management—the JV, the Chinese, and the foreign company— constitute one of the heads. The heads should have common goals and business directives, and they should share similar risks and financial burdens. But they don't. Each one has different strategies, motives, and time lines. The three heads are financially and legally joined at the hip, if you will, but with altogether different mind-sets.

I see the "monsters" when I'm hired by foreign companies to solve their JV problems. Consider, for example, one of my manufacturing clients, who for obvious reasons asked not to be named. The company produced high-end lighting fixtures in the United States and wanted to enter the lucrative hotel and office markets in China in the early '90s. At that time, most Chinese fixture manufacturers were producing low-end products not suitable for the new, lavish buildings going up in Shanghai. My client found a good deal with an SOE just outside of Shanghai. The SOE was already in the fixture business, so it already had equipment, infrastructure, experienced staff, and sales channels. They were losing money and so were very amenable to the prospect of finding a new partner—or rather, a new sugar daddy.

As with most JVs, things started out well. New steel-bending equipment was brought in, modern fixture designs were incorporated into the product mix, and sales soared. However, within five years, dozens of high-end fixture makers popped up into the market, cutting prices in half and slashing the JV's profits to almost nothing. They could barely say afloat. These competitors were smaller and more nimble than the state-run JV. The JV's goals, unbeknownst to its US owner, advocated full employment over profits, government and customer kickbacks over fair play, and creative accounting over GAAP (Generally Accepted Accounting Principles). The Chinese parent and JV management were all in it together, since the JV managers were all transfers from the mother company. Friends were supervising friends and filling each other's pockets. Of course, the US company had filled the JV's CEO and CFO positions with watchdog expatriates, but they were of little value. They could not communicate with their subordinates, instead having to rely on outside translators who themselves hardly knew any English. All information, translated documents, and reports were diluted and filtered before being sent to the round-eyed CEO and CFO.

The Chinese parent siphoned off funds in a very clever way. Though the JV factory had new or refurbished equipment, it kept breaking down, causing shortages of components. To make up for these bottlenecks, the JV purchased components at higher prices from another lighting fixture manufacturer across town— that just by coincidence, or not, was also owned by the Chinese parent company. They were, in effect, buying components from themselves. These occurrences increased every year to the point where over 50 percent of the bill of materials came from the Chinese parent's other factory. Later we found out through interviews with employees that they had purposely damaged the JV's equipment in order to force the JV to buy components from the other factory.

Within five years, bad management and corruption had left the JV in shambles, and the US partner wanted out. But a bigger problem arose. Chinese business law mandated that a unanimous board vote was needed to close down a JV—a fact my clients hadn't been aware of. The Chinese had three seats to the American's four seats. The two sides were locked. Time was on the Chinese side. As the stalemate lingered, the JV just continued to suck away at the American company's cash reserves.

This was about the time I stepped in. In actuality the resolution was simple, as it was clear what the Chinese wanted: money. The Chinese parent and JV management wanted compensation for their vote to dissolve the JV, so we made legal arrangements for the tradeoff and thought the nightmare was over. Not so fast. We made plans to ship back our equipment, but it got held up in customs. Apparently, the export documents, which needed the signatures of both JV owners, were missing. We went back to negotiate and made another arrangement for a tradeoff. After nine months (short for a JV wind-down), we received the equipment and final papers notifying the end of the JV legal entity. A lot of money was lost, but to look at the positive side—at least no one was arrested.

In other cases, I have seen Chinese parent companies transfer their least productive employees to, resell its used equipment or any excess inventory to, and dump bad accounting receivables to the JV. The JVs are treated like beaten-up stepchildren. One parent loves the child but lives too far away to care for him, while the other uses and abuses the child, pilfering away the monthly child support checks.

Chart 10.1 Setting Up in China

China Business Arrangement	Reasons to Do	Reasons Not to Do	Examples
Regional Distributors	1) Large customer base 2) Product needs on-site service	1) Channel conflict 2) Many partners to manage	Information technology, consumer products
Exclusive Distributor	1) Fewer, but larger customers 2) No channel conflict	Balance of power tilted towards distributor	Industrial and manufacturing equipment
Technology Licensing Partner	1) Involved in China with none of the hassles 2) Access to government-regulated industries	1) Intellectual property infringement 2) Never develop brand name 3) Never establish China business skills	Nanotechnology, pharmaceutical, aviation, medical equipment
Representative Office	1) Shows commitment to local customers 2) Can perform simple business activities	Cannot hire locals, invoice customers, manufacture products	Not recommended; other solutions have more advantages
Wholly Owned Foreign Enterprise (WOFE) – Sales	1) China business becomes significant 2) Need local employees	1) High start-up costs 2) Cumbersome laws and registration 3) Long-term commitment	Same as regional distributors
WOFE-Manufacturing	1) Lower costs 2) High import tariffs 3) China products are specialized 4) Long import lead times	1) Same reasons for WOFE-Sales 2) Intellectual property infringement	Automobile and industrial parts, electronics, low tech consumer goods
Joint Venture	Only for companies in government-regulated industries	Never do a joint venture unless absolutely necessary	Automobile, oil/gas, medical, biotech, aviation

Chapter 10 Summary

1. Eventually, foreign SMBs will outgrow their distributors. The next move is to set up a WOFE, which is basically a limited liability company registered in China.

2. With a WOFE, you can hire local employees, sell direct to customers, control sales and marketing activities, manufacture locally, and garner larger profits and sales.

3. WOFEs are a substantial investment, requiring a commitment of three to five years before seeing any profits. Many SMBs can't take the losses and bow out early.

4. The WOFE filing and registration process is cumbersome and time-consuming, sometimes taking up to two years for more complicated applications. Hire a local law firm to register your WOFE.

5. The location of your WOFE should be in close proximity to your customers. Chinese customers buy locally and pay cash.

6. SMBs almost always underestimate the initial WOFE setup costs. You can reduce expenses by hiring part-time workers, outsourcing accounting and human-resource functions, and using consultants like university professors.

7. Don't use headhunters to find your full-time employees. They are expensive and usually don't have a good inventory of

candidates. Rely on friends and word of mouth to find good, dependable, long-term employees.

8. Many WOFEs fail because of a lack of cohesiveness between the headquarters and its China subsidiary. SMBs should send their most trusted employees to China to integrate both the tangible functions (accounting, human resources, marketing) as well as the intangible ones (business philosophy, entrepreneurial culture, customer satisfaction).

9. Under no circumstances should an SMB do a Chinese JV. Even though you may be able to get majority ownership, you will be only a paper tiger, with the real control belonging to the Chinese parent company.

10. JVs are a three-headed monster, with each of the three managements—the JV, the Chinese parent company, and you—making up the heads. Each head has its own brain with self-motivating agendas.

Chapter 11
Thirteen Rules for Doing Business in China

As you can see by now, doing business in China can be a daunting task, so complicated that I (along with many others) can write books about it, and consulting companies and consultants can make their livelihoods on it. Many businesspeople say they can hardly take a holiday to China on their own—getting directions, ordering food, taking domestic flights—so how could they ever do business there? But don't think of it as one giant, insurmountable effort. Rather, as I have tried to do in this book, conquer China as a series of small steps. Take each action (conducting the market study, finding distributors, negotiating contracts, and so on) as a project in itself, and when each is accomplished, pat yourself on the back. Then move on to the next action item. Rome was not built in a day, nor will success in China be accomplished in a day. Think baby steps; and slowly, through perseverance, hard work, and stubbornness, you will get there, and it will be well worth your efforts.

Along with baby steps, it's vital to comprehend, remember, and emulate the concepts, lessons, and recommended actions that

I have discussed throughout this book. Though they are not a guaranteed formula for success, they will at least minimize your business risks and provide a blueprint for what to do and, more important, what not to do in China. My consulting stints for my successful clients normally last anywhere from two to five years, and in that time, the people I work with have heard my China sermons and eulogies a hundred times over and are full converts to my China business philosophies. Many hours have been spent with my clients in hotel restaurants in serious—sometimes heated—discussions about whether to do this or do that for their China strategies. I have spent many long nights negotiating across the table with corrupt, self-serving politicians who are acting as pseudo businesspeople and hoping a particular deal will eventually garner them a promotion back to Beijing. I have taken many long train rides to China's secondary cities, places that most Westerners have never heard of, to inspect a plastics factory, or purchase toilet seats, or tour an underground coal mine that probably lacked proper safety measures. Through all this, it is no wonder my consulting clients could probably recite my teachings verbatim.

But for most of you, the book's details may soon be a blur and only an afterthought as you engage with China. You will forget more than you will remember. It is for this reason that I have tried to summarize my thoughts and lessons into this final chapter with a set of short, simple rules. Everything I have written can be assigned to one or more of these easy-to-remember principles, so at the very least, tear out the pages from this chapter and review them as you are flying to Shanghai or Guangzhou, meeting with representatives from an SOE, or negotiating terms with that shrewd Chinese business owner. You just never know—it may save you a few million dollars.

Remember, these rules are meant to refresh your memory of the past chapters, not to be the final word or to be followed in exact terms. It would be wrong for a businessperson to go directly to this chapter without reading the previous ones and assume that doing business in China can be summed up in thirteen simplistic rules. It cannot. I have experienced exceptions to every one of my rules in past dealings with Chinese companies, so take each rule with a grain of salt. Use them as a foundation, but be flexible and ready to change tactics according to your specific business situation. I wish you the greatest luck and success in China and hope to hear from you about whether this book was of any value to your China endeavors.

Rule 1: Don't Rely on Gut Instincts

I accompany high-level managers to China. They have traveled all around the world, made dozens of successful deals, and met hundreds, if not thousands, of businesspeople. Of course, these successful businesspeople rely on facts and evidence to assist them in making business decisions. *Do we hire this person? Can we trust that person? Should we work with this company?* But more often than not, we seldom have all the facts to piece the puzzle together. If we did, business would be easy, a series of no-brainer decisions. But life isn't that simple, and that's why some businesspeople make the big bucks while others fail miserably. I think the successful ones, in the end, have better business instincts. Businesspeople often say things like, "I feel good about that person, so let's work with him," or "My gut tells me to do it this way." Whether you call it instinct, a sixth sense, or having a nose for business, it's this one quality that separates the men from the boys and the women from the girls.

I have no doubt Western businesspeople can sometimes make accurate decisions partially or even wholly on instincts. An

American for example, could make a fairly accurate judgment on another American, although a complete stranger, regarding his or her past, character, and trustworthiness. In fact, I'll even go as far as conceding that an American could "make a gut call" on other Westerners, say a German or Englishman, and vice versa, since many Western countries share similar religions, histories, education systems, moral and ethical standards, and legal practices.

But your gut won't work in China. Westerners just don't share as much in common with the Chinese as they do with their fellow Westerners. You don't watch the same television shows, eat the same foods, or speak the same language, so why should you think the same? You don't. So don't think you can see through them or make instinctive and accurate judgments about Chinese businesspeople or situations.

When I worked at Philips Electronics in my early twenties, I traveled all over Asia doing business with Indians, Indonesians, and Koreans, among others, and I could never accurately predict their next moves or understand why they made certain business decisions. This was partly due to language barriers, but it was mostly due to cultural differences: how we saw the world, how we viewed success, and how local norms expected us to behave. As I was young and inexperienced, I accepted these differences, realized I would never fully understand my foreign counterparts, and relied heavily on local Philips employees to guide me. Too embarrassed to admit my shortcomings, I blindly followed my local colleagues, often making business decisions that seemingly didn't make sense at first but ultimately proved successful. I followed other people's gut instincts.

But my clients today are usually older businesspeople in their fifties and sixties. With age comes experience and the belief that you've seen and done everything already. When these elder statesmen and women go to China for the first time, they treat it like any other country they have tackled in the past. It is difficult for me to get across to them that China, having no Western heritage, is a completely different animal. Sometimes my most difficult task is to convince my clients to erase from their minds everything they've previously done, clean the slate, and go to China with an open mind. It's hard to do, and few can actually manage it.

The few businesspeople who can admit ignorance about China have a much better chance of success. They go to China without any pretense, prejudices, or expectations. They don't pass judgment on anyone or any situation. They rely on facts, not a sixth sense, to make decisions. And when the facts fall short, their egos will allow them to defer to experts to make those gut calls.

Rule 2: You Don't Know What You Don't Know

I cannot claim ownership of the sentiment "You don't know what you don't know." I first heard it from one of my consulting clients one night when we were discussing a potential distributorship with a local Chinese company. Casually over dinner, my fifty-five-year-old client asked me to briefly describe the differences between working with Chinese distributors as opposed to Western distributors. He expected some short, trite answer, as we were finishing up our decadent sesame ball dessert before heading to bed. I sarcastically replied, "You got all night?" He didn't believe me at first. We subsequently spent the next four hours going over the differences. At the end of the marathon session, he sheepishly said, "I can't believe there's so much I don't know. In fact, there's so much I don't know, I don't even know what I don't know."

He was my first consulting client. It dawned on me after what he said that I could actually run a business helping Western companies with their China strategies. As I began meeting with small businesses wanting to go to China, most were very open in admitting they knew little about China and accepted a steep learning curve to get up to speed. They hired me as their resident China expert but with one caveat: I had to do things on their terms. Sure, I had free rein to select Chinese distributors, but I was told how many distributors to hire. I could decide where to start a WOFE, but I was explicitly told how many employees to hire. I could decide who to sell to, but I was told what price to set.

I tend to find this "do as you wish, but under my directions" attitude more prevalent with SMBs than with larger companies. I think it's because entrepreneurs do everything on their own and are not accustomed to relying on consultants or experts, whereas larger companies often hire subject-matter experts specializing in one area or another. A large company, for example, will hire one accountant to handle accounts receivable and another one for accounts payable. An SMB will just use one accountant for everything—receivables, payables, payroll, and taxes.

SMBs have to change their attitudes if they want to find success in China. Yes, they know what they don't know, and they use me to find distributors, set up WOFEs, or negotiate contracts. I solve their *who, what, when, where,* and *why* questions. After filling in the missing pieces, however, SMBs assume they know the rest, and I then become a messenger rather than a true consultant. I just do as I'm told. Or worse yet, many clients let me go, assuming they can cover things from there. But they don't realize that a hundred more questions hide behind the *who* question. *Are they private or state-owned? Can they be a future competitor? An exclusive or regional partner?*

Chart 11.1 shows some of the additional questions I ask on basic business issues that Westerners typically omit. The left-out issues are not normally relevant in the West, but they are paramount when dealing with the Chinese. Take, for example, outsourcing. Most Westerners are satisfied visiting the principal manufacturer, not realizing that additional trips are needed to visit the raw materials and subcomponents factories as well. I also insist that my outsourcing clients patent or trademark their products and brand names in China even though the products are shipped back to the West, for fear that the outsourcing factory will sell knockoffs locally.

My most important task as a China consultant is to make my clients aware of the unknowns concerning China—to make them think about the things they normally would not consider when doing business in the West. Before a Chinese business trip, I always recite to myself, "I don't know what I don't know." It keeps me humble and on my toes, makes me ask more questions of others and myself, and most of all, keeps my customers out of trouble in China.

Chart 11.1 The Important Questions Not Asked by Westerners

Subject	Relevant Questions Often Not Asked
Outsourcing	1) Are your suppliers using shadow factories? 2) How do we check our partners' suppliers for quality? 3) How do we know approved materials are being used? 4) Will they sell knockoffs to other customers?
Selling to China	1) Should we introduce lower-priced products? 2) Would it be better to sell older or earlier generation products? 3) Are there local competitors? 4) Is this a government-controlled industry?
Contracts	1) How else can we protect ourselves? 2) Have all trust-related issues been taken out of the contract? 3) Will contract disputes hold up in Chinese court?
Choosing Partners	1) Are they state-owned or privately owned? 2) Do they have regional or national coverage? 3) Are we creating a competitor? 4) How do we prove everything they say?

Rule 3: Sweat the Details

Many SMB owners are entrepreneurs and risk takers, preferring to take action first and ask questions later. This philosophy can have dire consequences in China. I have personally witnessed thousands of hours' worth of software code and millions of dollars' worth of intellectual property lost to the Chinese by SMBs making brash, uninformed, and shoot-from-the-hip decisions. You will not only lose your China business, but you could potentially be risking everything you worked for in your home country. In the United States, we can recover from our mistakes through a variety of methods: sue a competitor for patent infringement, spend more on advertising, or meet face-to-face with disgruntled customers. It's harder to recover from mistakes in China.

So don't make mistakes—or at least minimize them. I do this by sweating the details before going to China. I do everything possible before my client outsources their first widget or sells their first product to China. I think the whole process through. The key is to take all assumptions out of your China action plan. Don't assume a distributor is trustworthy; rather, take the trust factor out and make them earn it. Start the relationship off with cash-only payment terms, no exclusivity, and stiff quarterly quotas. Don't assume a Chinese contract protects you; consult with different lawyers, review legal trends, seek alternatives like arbitration versus going to court, and have backup plans to protect yourself. For example, a high-tech products company may not want to sell its state-of-the-art technologies to China. Chinese customers may be just as happy with older but less-expensive technologies, thereby protecting intellectual property and creating a cash cow for the already fully depreciated technology assets.

Once all assumptions have been accounted for and we have come close to a definitive action plan, I then go through a final "what if" analysis. I consider all possible scenarios. *What if we fail? What if government regulations change? What if this happens? What if that happens?* I then detail a contingency plan, keeping it in my back pocket to use when needed. This analysis should cover all your bases and allow for multiple action plans from month to month. Remember, actions plans will change as the China business climate alters, whether it's new banking regulations, import tariffs, industry restrictions, or anything else. You are prepared for these sudden gyrations through your assumptions and "what if" scenario playing.

Rule 4: Take the Trust Factor Out
We rely so much on trust in our business dealings. We want to trust our business partners, customers, suppliers, and employees.

I learned about the four Ps in business school: product, price, place, and promotion. Since trust is so important in business, it should almost be considered the fifth P. Not so in China; trust must be completely taken out of the equation. Everything you do with a Chinese company should be proven, preferably by a third party or by your own eyes and ears. I believe this for several reasons. First, China is still a developing country and its people, particularly the Mao Generation, are one or two generations behind Western ethical and moral codes. China will eventually become Westernized as their standards of living rise, the educational system evolves, the government becomes less corrupt, and its people travel abroad more frequently. Today, however, the vast majority of Chinese still struggle to make ends meet and worry about their future nest egg. The Mao Generation will get every dollar they can with little regard to how they get it or who they have to cheat to get it.

Another reason is that corruption in China is a daily event. We see it at the national level: high-ranking politicians caught receiving bribes or holding overseas slush funds with millions of dollars; state-owned drug companies paying off Chinese FDA officials. We see it at the provincial level: construction companies paying off local officials for use of public property to build high-rise apartments; babies sold off to illegal adoption agencies for resale. And we see it at the local level: immigrants buying fake government identification cards; speeding motorists paying off cops on the take. I don't give any excuses for my Chinese business partners, but I can understand why they might engage in illicit activities. Seeing this stuff everyday makes you immune to it, and to some extent, makes it seem more okay to do. *If the government does it, then why can't I? If the police do it, then why can't I?*

Taking the trust factor out of any business relationship is, however, easier said than done. Trust is such a big part of our Western business philosophy. We trust that our employees are working eight-hour days when they work at home, and we believe our contract manufacturers are using preapproved components. This is not necessarily so in China. Make sure your distributors are who they say they are. Confirm that the raw materials used in your made-in-China products are the ones you specified. And check to see that your Chinese employees aren't selling trade secrets to your competitors.

Rule 5: Never Do JVs

Except for certain regulated industries in China, JVs are a thing of the past. As China was developing and shaping its pseudo market economy in the 1970s, it forced all multinationals to form JVs with SOEs. The reasons were twofold. First, SOEs were antiquated, void of new technologies, and served as welfare systems for their employees and local politicians. Only by working with foreign companies could they get up to speed in learning and in obtaining new management styles, technologies, and ingenuity. Second, Beijing didn't trust foreigners, nor did they want foreign companies to take over the domestic market with superior goods and services. JVs were somewhat of a comprise; they allowed the large multinationals a piece of China's enormous consumer market even as they were being controlled, manipulated, and kept under the watchful eye of the state government. MNOs had no choice but to accept these terms. It was either the Communist way or the highway.

Conditions and regulations are much better today. For the most part, almost any foreign company, large or small, can freely set up its own operation without the hassles of a JV (as long as it does not operate in one of the regulated industries). This frees foreign enterprises of many past inconveniences: intellectual property theft, training and nurturing future competitors, dealing with JV management and boards, income and profit dilution, and good old-fashioned strong-arming from local, better-connected, government-controlled partners.

Given all these advantages, why on earth would any foreign company want to do a JV? Those in favor of it—and there are still many—claim JVs have upsides: they mitigate risks; bring in local expertise, knowledge, and government contacts; require lower investments; and open up more market opportunities. I am sorry, but I just don't believe any of it. For one, foreign companies can hire ex-government officials and business executives for local knowledge, contacts, and market opportunities. Second, a company should never go to China in the first place if it can't stomach the risk, investments, and day-to-day market gyrations. Finally, going to a China is a full commitment, not a halfhearted side bet. You are either in or out. If you are out, that's okay, but stay clear away. If you are in, then jump in with 100 percent conviction, prepared to put in maximum time, effort, and money. JVs are for wimps who want to dabble in China—and dabbling doesn't create success in China.

Rule 6: Adapt and Move Quickly

Every six months or so, I visit lawyers in China to get updates on both national and local business regulations. I'm amazed by all the changes that take can place in such a short period, such as different import duties, new WOFE regulations, increased hourly labor rates, and changes in the corporate tax structure.

Changes that may take years in the United States can take only weeks in China. New laws and regulations can be made almost instantaneously.

Market conditions can change even faster, some due to natural supply-and-demand factors and others due to government intervention. Due to overharvesting of cabbage in 2011, cabbage prices plummeted from about six US cents per kilogram to just one cent in less than one growing season. Prices for rare earth metals shot up in 2010 when China blocked shipments to Japan in retaliation over an island dispute. An SMB sensitive to fluctuations in prices and raw material shortages must always anticipate these changes and adapt to them quickly and decisively.

Imagine any one of the following hypothetical events in China: China retaliates against President Obama's incessant demands for China to allow the renminbi to appreciate by setting restrictions on the amount of capital that can be repatriated back to the United States. China suddenly raises the minimum labor rates by 20 percent and requires companies to pay for more social welfare benefits to their employees. Taxi drivers and truck drivers go on a national strike to protest rising fuel prices. If events like these occur, an SMB must react quickly and not assume these are just fly-by-night occurrences that will go away tomorrow. They will not. I have witnessed many companies make the mistake of trying to wait the problem out or avoid doing anything about it. Analyze the situation, weigh the choices, and take action at the speed of light.

Rule 7: Never Compete with Locals

SMBs come to me with many different types of products and services to offer to China. I reject four out of every five business offerings mostly because China either already has similar products or services or because Chinese competitors can easily duplicate them. Foreign players can never match a local Chinese competitor's cost, speed to market, flexibility, and all-around customer and market intelligence. Remember, you are on someone else's turf, and locals will always have their advantages, just as you know your local market (pricing, customers, market) better than outsiders ever will.

An SMB's cost structure alone will be an inhibiting factor for success in China. Let's say a foreign SMB and a local competitor make exactly the same product in the same city and sell to the same customers, leaving cost as the only variable. The foreign company will always have at least 30 to 40 percent higher costs than the local company. Locals don't have to deal with costs associated with WOFE setup, expatriates, English-speaking employees, and headquarter overhead. And these are just the legitimate expenses. Local Chinese companies often cheat on taxes, hire undocumented workers, and are lax about safety regulations, while foreign companies stick to the rules and pay through their noses.

So always examine your products and services carefully, making sure no Chinese competitors exist. More importantly, before going to China, make sure your business offerings cannot be easily pirated in China or else you may lose more than just China—you might put your whole business in jeopardy.

Rule 8: Use Multiple Partners
When selling to China, I never offer exclusivity to Chinese agents, licensing partners, or distributors. Too much can and will go wrong. First, I would be breaking rule #2. Exclusivity requires a

foreign SMB to put trust in its Chinese partner, giving them full control, autonomy, and authority in all of China. Being halfway around the world, you wouldn't have any firsthand market information, and you'll end up having to depend solely on your partner. What price is the partner selling at? Who are they selling to? Are they pirating the products?

Second, exclusivity becomes a lose-lose situation. If business is poor, you're stuck with a bad partner for the remainder of the contract period. If business is great, the Chinese partner can essentially blackmail you. They control all aspects of your China business—pricing, customers, marketing, and distribution—and thus can demand better terms or cut you off.

Third, China is just too big of a country for one partner. Rarely do you see one distributor having exclusivity in the United States, so why offer exclusivity to an even larger, more fragmented country like China? On top of that, Chinese companies tend to concentrate their efforts in one region of the country; a Beijing distributor will handle the northeast, a Shenzhen agent controls the south, and a Shanghai licensee sells in the east. Each company has strengths in its region, so use that to your advantage.

There are a number of key advantages to having multiple partners. Each partner will keep a watchful eye on the others to lessen the possibility of cheating or pirating. Pricing will be kept in check, preventing excessive profits and maximizing unit sales. Relative performance can be tracked and measured, enabling you to weed out the bad ones. And different sales and marketing tactics can be tested with different partners in different regions, with the more profitable strategies later being applied to the whole country.

The same goes when outsourcing from China: use multiple vendors from different cities. This allows you to compare prices, quality, lead times, and service. Especially in today's rocky economic climate, Chinese companies come and go, and you don't want to be caught with your pants down with an outsourcing partner on the brink of going belly-up. In the past few years, China has lost thousands of toy factories, hundreds of heavy industrial equipment manufacturers, and dozens of solar module producers. If an SMB is already in China selecting an outsourcing partner, then it usually doesn't take that much more effort to qualify a second one. The audit processes are the same, requiring only a few extra days and domestic fights.

Rule 9: Think Long-Term but React Short-Term

For China, SMBs must have both short-term actions and long-term strategies or goals. These two concepts are very different. China is in a constant state of flux, so companies cannot just sit around and maintain the status quo. Short-term actions are not necessarily well-thought-out or planned activities. Rather, they are actions and reactions based on changes in economic, political, or legal conditions affecting your business. You may make these moves daily, monthly, or weekly. Also, when in China, SMBs will encounter many interesting people, situations, threats, and opportunities. Act and react to these events. Seize opportunities when they arise, look beyond the obvious, don't underestimate who can do things for you, and don't take local competitors lightly.

Here is one example of what I mean: When I was developing the PC memory market for Kingston Technology in the mid-1990s, I wanted to find the large, well-known information technology distributors throughout China and Asia. They had name-brand recognition, money, contacts, thousands of employees, and logistic offices everywhere. Bigger was better—or so I thought at that time. My efforts were focused on working with the giants like Ingram Micro China and Tech Data China.

As I traveled in China to various trade shows, many small, five-to-seven-employee, mom-and-pop distributors would approach me, asking to distribute Kingston memory. I laughed at them. *What a joke!* I thought. *There's no way we want to work with these small guys. What can they do for us?* But they were persistent and kept contacting me. Then one day, a small Wuhan distributor, whom I met previously, called and said he had a potential $1 million memory order in the pipeline. I sarcastically replied, "Send the purchase order, wire the funds, and then we'll talk." *I'm not going to hear back from this joker.*

To make a long story short, he came through with the order and many more over the years. I never looked a gift horse in the mouth again in China. That one "nobody" from Wuhan changed my thinking about China. As I learned over the years, these smaller, nimble players are simply hungrier and faster. The owners concentrate their time in one city only; sell only a few, select products; and have a strong, loyal customer base. They are tough to beat. Since then, I have always taken the opportunity to meet anybody anywhere, no matter how big or small. Success can come in many packages.

I look at long-term goals as where you want to be in the next five to seven years in China. These plans are not the sum total of all the short-term actions, but instead, they are personal aspirations and views of what your China business should look like in the future. They're what make you work hard and continue to chip away in China. I like to set revenue goals for my clients. For clients selling to China, I would like their China sales to be 20 to 25 percent of their total net sales in five to seven years. It's a fair number given the amount of time, money, and opportunity cost a company will give up in that period. Of course, the specific goals and numbers will vary for each company and industry, but I challenge my customers to set high but realistic long-term goals.

Rule 10: Don't Create Competitors

Chinese companies are the best copycats in the world; I don't mean that necessarily in a negative way, though many Western companies, victimized by Chinese pirating, may think otherwise. In the eighties, the Chinese made crude, easily discernible, low-tech fakes of Gucci bags and Nike sneakers. In the nineties we saw better, more realistic copies of Rolex watches and Calloway golf clubs. Today we don't just see knockoffs that are perfectly made, in both appearance and functionality, of Apple iPods and Macintosh computers, but we've also seen an actual, full-blown Apple store replicated in Kunming. Even the employees, who sported the same blue Apple shirts and nametags, thought they were working in a real, legitimate Apple outlet. I was also bamboozled when I thought I was driving a Mercedes-Benz CLS Class through the outskirts of Shanghai. It turned out to be a fake, but an excellent one it was. The smoothness of the ride, the changing of gears, and the perfectly crafted doors were actually like the authentic ones.

These examples of pirating are downright mind-boggling and technically impressive, yet at the same time, scary. They are mind-boggling because they show how the Chinese are evolving from "research and copy" to "research and develop." Pirated goods are now exact replicas. The next step will be to design and manufacture products that are better in appearance, functionality, and cost than the originals. This shift is scary because the Chinese are doing it right under our noses, with our permission; this comes in the forms of aircraft engine joint ventures, nanotechnology license agreements, and joint biomedical R&D projects using China's cheap professional workforce.

And we Westerners still haven't learned our lessons. We gave away high-speed rail technologies twenty years ago, automotive technologies ten years ago, and now are doing the same for the aerospace industry. Western aerospace companies are gladly handing over their intellectual property to do business with COMAC, the new commercial aircraft manufacturing company in China. The Chinese government has mandated that all foreign companies must form joint ventures with Chinese state-owned enterprises if they wish to sell products or services to COMAC. This is becoming a vicious cycle: we give our secrets away and then complain about it, forget it ever happened, and then do it all over again. When will it stop?

Rule 11: Listen to Experts

Foreign SMBs pay me handsomely for advice on China, follow me for weeks to the oddest places in China, and ask me to present my findings to their owners or board of directors. After all this, half will usually take me up on my recommendations or at least implement my core findings, tweaking things here and there. The half that listen to me know they need experts, because they have already failed in China; they went it alone and took a beating. Only after a humbling experience do most SMBs realize they need experts to help them with China.

The other half, the companies that completely discard and ignore my results, are still newcomers to China. They hire me to get some tidbits about China and then independently go their way. The decision to use a consultant like me is usually made at the very top, by a CEO or owner; they will interview me, hire me, and ask me to work with their executive teams to carve out a China plan. It's these executives who are very much against working with me. They are all seasoned businesspeople who already have had success with various companies, have worked as expatriates in foreign countries, and sometimes speak several foreign languages. They feel they don't need a consultant for China and view my presence as an insult—or worse, as a threat. I can't help those who don't want to be helped.

These companies who reject outside China experts often simply "don't know what they don't know." However, once they get burned, lose money, or are cheated, they realize all the unknowns China has to offer, and then I (or another China expert) will be there to bail them out. Don't make the mistake of blindly going to China, and don't make the mistake of treating China just like any other country. Use consultants or hire seasoned, China business professionals, and most important, listen to what they have to say. Do it the right way the first time.

Rule 12: Don't Rely on Contracts

There are two reasons contracts cannot be relied on in China. First, contracts do not have the same meaning in China as they do in the West. For the Chinese, the contract is more of a symbolic gesture, the start of good things to come. And because contracts are symbolic, many Chinese feel they can change the terms of the contract at any time. To them it's just an agreed-upon set of terms for today based on today's market conditions. If an American partner is outsourcing actuator motors from a Chinese supplier, for example, the factory agrees to prices based on today's raw material, fuel, and shipping costs. The Chinese, however, feel they have an inalienable right to raise prices later when market conditions change, even though the original price is guaranteed for two years. Remember, however, that it goes both ways. The Chinese have no qualms about their Western partners wanting to change the terms as well.

With this said, however, things are getting better. Chinese companies, especially SOEs, have come a long way from the 1970s and '80s when they first started signing contracts with Western companies. More and more Chinese enterprises synchronize their mind-sets to the West when writing, negotiating, and following contracts. Now Chinese companies are taking more time to review contracts; in the past, they signed virtually anything without reading it. And they are well aware that contract terms must be upheld throughout the length of the contract. I have had several dealings where Chinese SMBs have delayed contract signings so they could double-check the contract details, making sure they could uphold the terms. This shows how serious the Chinese are now with contracts. I suspect that in the next twenty years, as the Chinese become even more Westernized and with the further maturation of Chinese law, that the Chinese will treat contracts with equal reverence and weight as Westerners.

The second reason contracts cannot be relied on is the lack of enforceability in China. There's little chance a foreign SMB will win in court over another Chinese SMB, and there's zero chance an SMB will win over an SOE. Local SMBs will fold up before they ever walk into a courtroom, and the Chinese judicial system and SOEs are essentially one and the same. They all report to the same boss: Beijing. Remember, no separation of powers exists in China. Everything is controlled by the Communist Party. The party is the government, and they have the final say in the courts.

Rule 13: When in Doubt, Ask Questions

Too often I have returned from a China trip with my Western clients only to have them come back to me with a hundred questions that could have been easily answered during our face-to-face meetings in China, but they were too shy, polite, or jet-lagged to ask. Maybe they simply didn't want to be nosy. I don't know, maybe it's the food or the air. For whatever reason, Westerners become quiet in China. Meetings in China are difficult. Conversations are fragmented and interrupted with translations. Many people are talking at the same time. Discussion topics can go astray and wander. And the Chinese, when speaking in broken English, are difficult to comprehend. It can be very frustrating, especially for first-timers to China. But you are in China to get a job done and to collect data. So ask if you don't understand. Ask the same question again if it still wasn't answered or if it was misinterpreted. And do it again and again until you are totally satisfied. Most businesspeople consider that impolite, but I would rather be rude than have to leave China with inconclusive data and wrong assumptions.

Another reason to ask questions is that your potential Chinese partners will often leave out key information that is vital to your decision making. It's not that they do this intentionally. Chinese people tend to speak in generalities, not getting down to the specifics. They often won't get the gist of your question and will give broad, sweeping answers in response. So don't ask general questions like "Can you explain your quality processes?" or "What is your sales strategy?" This will lead nowhere except to generic rhetoric. Rather, ask pointed questions as if you were a lawyer cross-examining a key witness. For example, here's a line of questioning I would enlist to understand the quality process in a syringe factory: *What constitutes a bad syringe? What do you do when you find a bad syringe? What tests do you perform? Can I see a sample report? What preventative measures did you take? Can you take me through a recent real-life example? May I speak to the people who handled this case?* True, these questions are intimidating and uncomfortable, and may even be a bit insulting. But that's okay. The Chinese can handle and accept tough love—it's nothing the Mao Generation didn't go through during the Cultural Revolution. The fifty-something Chinese bosses and managers are accustomed to such interrogations. The bottom line is that these hard-line questions will get to the truth and constitute the basis of your China action plan.

The Chinese also *unintentionally*—though foreigners may think otherwise—misrepresent themselves, so it's important to ask questions either to confirm your assumptions or to clarify their accidental inferences. A few examples will make this point clear. Chinese distributors print both the names of their own companies and the companies they represent on their business cards. An Osram lighting distributor, for example, will put Osram in bold red letters on their cards. Foreigners can easily mistake the distributor for the actual European lighting manufacturer. The same goes for distributors for Philips, General Electric, and dozens of other international companies. Make sure you know whom you are dealing with. Distributors will also boast about the many sales offices and employees they have scattered about China. However, in most cases, these are only resellers, having no more than a buy-sell relationship. Ask to visit these "subsidiary" offices, meet the employees, and again, cross-examine them to the bone.

In 2009 when a client of mine, an American testing company for aircraft systems and parts, first visited COMAC, we met with a vice director we thought was in charge of the engineering of their new C919 regional jet aircraft. He sure played the part; he answered all of our questions regarding the new aircraft, asked engineering managers to attend our meeting, and aligned us with internal engineering departments for future discussions. We failed to get anywhere, and we later learned that he was in charge of infrastructure (the management and buildup of COMAC's new buildings) and had nothing to do with the research and development groups. True, he had certainly led us to believe he was *the man*, but we had ourselves to blame as well. Our line of questioning, which assumed he was indeed the man in charge, may have left him too embarrassed to admit otherwise. And of course, we didn't ask the $6 million question: Are you in charge of the C919 project? Never assume. Never leave any stone unturned. Ask questions no matter how rude or how trivial they may seem.

22880496R00142

Made in the USA
Lexington, KY
18 May 2013